MW00323556

CONTACT YOUR GUARDIAN ANGEL

TRANSFORM YOUR LIFE

PAUL ROLAND

quantum

LONDON • NEW YORK • TORONTO • SYDNEY

quantum

An imprint of W. Foulsham & Co. Ltd
The Publishing House, Bennetts Close, Cippenham, Slough,
Berkshire, SL1 5AP, England

ISBN 0-572-03047-9

Copyright © 2005 Paul Roland

Cover illustration by Jurgen Ziewe

Photograph on page 30 reproduced from the Kabbalah Cards by
permission of AGM AGMüller Urania, Bahnhofstrasse 21, CH-8212
Neuhasen am Rheinfall, Switzerland

A CIP record for this book is available from the British Library

The moral right of the author has been asserted

All rights reserved

The Copyright Act prohibits (subject to certain very
limited exceptions) the making of copies of any
copyright work or of a substantial part of such a work,
including the making of copies by photocopying or
similar process. Written permission to make a copy or
copies must therefore normally be obtained from the
publisher in advance. It is advisable also to consult the
publisher if in any doubt as to the legality of any
copying which is to be undertaken.

Disclaimer: The exercises in this book are intended for increasing
self-awareness. However, if you have recently experienced psychological
problems or are taking prescribed medication you should seek
professional medical advice before practising meditation. Neither the
editors of W. Foulsham & Co. Ltd nor the author nor the publisher take
responsibility for any possible consequences from any treatment,
procedure, test, exercise, action or application of medication or
preparation by any person reading or following the information in this
book. The publication of this book does not constitute the practice of
medicine, and this book does not attempt to replace any diet or
instructions from your doctor. The author and publisher advise the
reader to check with a doctor before administering any medication or
undertaking any course of treatment or exercise.

Printed in Great Britain by Creative Print & Design (Wales), Ebbw Vale

Contents

With love and gratitude to Jill Nash, an angel in human form.

Introduction

This is an 'angel' book with a difference. And it's a crucial difference. *You do not need to believe in angels in order to benefit from the insights and exercises in this book.* To be more precise, you do not need to believe that angels are celestial messengers in idealised human form equipped with wings and a halo.

Although there is overwhelming anecdotal evidence to indicate the existence of benign discarnate beings, there is no irrefutable proof that angels exist in the form with which we in the West are familiar. And frankly, it is not necessary to provide any. All spiritual experience is subjective. For that reason no one, not even the self-proclaimed New Age angel gurus, is qualified to make a definitive statement regarding the nature of angels and I shall certainly not be making one myself.

Part of the problem, I suspect, is that in this day and age the idea of each of us having a guardian angel seems just too good to be true. We demand irrefutable proof before we put our faith in anything and we demand it in a form that we can recognise. We therefore tend to dismiss the angels' subtle but significant influence in our lives as mere coincidence or good luck. We behave like the devoutly religious man in the joke who is clinging on to the cliff edge by his fingertips and praying to God to send an angel to rescue him. Within a few minutes a helicopter happens past and offers to help but the man refuses, assuring the pilot that God is going to send an angel. The helicopter turns back and a few minutes later a speedboat comes by. 'Jump into the water,' shouts the pilot, 'I'll pull you in.' Again, the old man politely refuses assuring the pilot that he is expecting an angel to pull him to safety. Finally, an eager boy scout appears at the cliff edge and peering down offers to go and get a rope. Again, the old man refuses. Ten minutes later he loses his grip, plunges fifty metres into the sea and drowns. His spirit ascends to heaven and there he comes face to face with his Creator.

'Lord, why did you forsake me. I prayed for an angel to help me, but it never came.'

'I hear all prayers,' God replies. 'I sent a helicopter, a speedboat and a boy scout, but you refused help from all of them.'

I have had many extraordinary experiences which have convinced me of the existence of angels, some of which I have described in the following pages. To these I have added the remarkable insights of several psychics, mediums and healers with whom I have had the pleasure of working over the years. But the real proof will come when you explore the other realities for yourself. In the later chapters of this book I offer various methods you can use to connect with your guardian angel and I conclude with several advanced techniques for exploring the upper worlds of the angelics so that you can evaluate the experiences for yourself.

It is not important what names you apply to the various energies you will experience, nor is it necessary for you to see an angel in the course of your visualisations, although it is highly likely that you will. What is important is that you develop an increasing sense of their presence and that you benefit in subtle but significant ways from their unseen influence.

Neither will it be necessary for you to study a hierarchy of spiritual beings and commit their names, divine attributes and duties to memory. A lot of New Age nonsense has been written about the nature of angels, their supposed powers, their place in the heavenly hierarchy and how you can ask them to provide you with a parking space whenever you require one. My understanding of the nature of angels is that they are a sublime expression of the Divine and those who experience a visitation are blessed and profoundly affected for the rest of their lives. To view these benign beings as our celestial servants is the height of human arrogance and, besides, it demeans us in the process because it affirms the false belief that we are powerless puppets at the whim of fate and it delegates responsibility for our development to an outside agency. We alone are responsible for our spiritual development for we are, in a sense, angels in the making.

As a qualified counsellor and spiritual teacher I am opposed to anything which does not empower individuals to help themselves, to become more self-aware and take control of their own lives. It is right that we should acknowledge the assistance of angels and spirit guides, but if we make the mistake of worshipping them, then we deny our true, divine nature which distinguishes us from the angels, for we can exercise free will which they, apparently, cannot.

As you work through the practical exercises please do not be tempted to skip the basic techniques. Meditation is the foundation of all spiritual and psychic work. It will help to ground you, to establish a strong connection with the higher self and to enable you to expand your awareness beyond the confines of the body and return safely with insights that will enrich your everyday life. Before you can explore other dimensions and other realities, you need to be able to quieten your mind so that you can distinguish between what is imagination and what is a genuine communication. Angels apparently have the ability to appear spontaneously at a dramatic moment in our lives leaving a profound sense of the Divine, but if we want to be able to contact them whenever we need guidance or help, we have to climb Jacob's Ladder one rung at a time.

1

Frequently Asked Questions about Angels

During the many angel workshops which I have given over the years I have found that there are a dozen or so questions which are asked at almost every session. So, I thought it would be useful to answer them here and in so doing clear up some popular misconceptions before we go any further.

What evidence is there that angels exist?

There is overwhelming anecdotal evidence to suggest that some form of benign discarnate being does exist and that these beings can and do take an active interest in our lives. Some of the most convincing cases are presented in the following pages. But even if you have not seen an angel, you will have been touched by one in some way at a significant moment or moments in your life.

Take the opportunity right now to count your blessings, as they used to say. Can you honestly attribute all of these to good luck and hard work? The exercises in this book are designed to raise your awareness of these incidents of angelic intervention and to enable you to make contact with your guardian angel at will.

What exactly is an angel?

That is one of the main questions that I intend to answer with the help of several experienced psychics and healers who claim to have had a personal encounter with the angels. Their experiences together with my own insights will, I hope, shed new light on the nature and purpose of angels and dispel some of the more fanciful misconceptions that have persisted both in religious and New Age mythology.

Everybody's experience is different and is coloured by their religious background, their beliefs and to an extent their upbringing. My understanding is that angels are an expression of the Divine, a personification of a higher frequency of energy.

What is the difference between a spirit guide and an angel?

The common definition of a spirit guide is a discarnate soul who has chosen to assist the living from the world of spirit rather than reincarnating to experience another life on earth. Guides usually appear in an archetypal form connected with healing or esoteric wisdom such as a Native American or Chinese. I suspect this is merely the way in which we perceive these personalities who are devoid of form, being pure consciousness.

An angel has an entirely different nature. It is an inhabitant of the upper worlds and is, in a sense, incomplete in that it does not possess free will but exists to facilitate the processes of evolution. Above these 'lesser angels' are the archangels who are known by name and who embody specific attributes of the Creator.

I have heard that there is a heavenly hierarchy that comprises of various classes of angels with specific powers, namely the thrones, dominions, principalities, powers and virtues. Is it necessary for me to learn all of these?

Absolutely not! I find the whole idea of a heavenly hierarchy where angels are ranked like policemen to be ludicrous and fanciful in the extreme. This myth originated from a misinterpretation of St Paul's letter to the Ephesians in the New Testament, which has been perpetuated by those angel 'experts' who feel the need to see the universe as conforming to human rules.

In the letter St Paul reminds the new converts that God is on their side.

> 'For by God were all things created that are in heaven,
> and that are in earth, visible and invisible, whether they
> be thrones or dominions, or principalities, or powers:
> all things were created by him, and for him.' (Col 1:16)

It is obvious that the thrones, dominions, principalities and powers to which he refers are not individual ranks in an angelic hierarchy, but rather symbols of temporal power on earth. 'Thrones' refers to all rulers whose power is transient and 'dominions' to a land governed by a single ruler or an elected body. A principality is a region ruled by a prince, while 'powers' would cover all other forms of authority. St Paul is clearly listing terrestrial authorities in order of descent. He makes no explicit reference in the passage to angels and, in fact, makes the analogy between terrestrial and celestial power even clearer in a previous passage.

> *'Far above all principality, and power, and might, and dominion, and every name that is named, not only in this world, but also in that which is to come...[is God.]' (Eph 1:21)*

In an earlier letter he makes a further distinction between angels and the temporal symbols of power.

> *'For I am persuaded that neither death, nor life, nor angels, nor principalities, nor powers, nor things present, nor things to come; Nor height, nor depth, nor any other creature, shall be able to separate us from the love of God.' (Rom 8:38–39)*

This leaves the virtues mentioned in medieval angelology which, I suggest, are simply the cardinal virtues of prudence, justice, fortitude and temperance personified by early theologians as the divine attributes latent in man.

I suggest that it is not only misleading but also irresponsible for anyone to make statements of fact concerning a supposed angel hierarchy unless they can claim to have journeyed personally to heaven and taken a roll-call of each angel's name and job description!

Does everybody have a guardian angel?

It would appear so, but I would suggest that our guardian angel and what the mystics call our higher self may be one and the same. Much of the intuitive guidance we receive is indicative of a phenomenon known as channelling, which occurs when we are receptive to messages from the unconscious or what orthodox religion might call our conscience.

The original meaning of the word 'genius' (derived from the Latin *gignere* 'to create') was a reference to an individual's guardian spirit, which gave rise to the idea that inspiration was a form of angelic blessing. But it is my understanding that it was this immortal aspect, which Jesus referred to when he said, 'The kingdom of heaven is within you', and which Siddhartha Gautama, the Buddha, acknowledged as the Buddha nature in us all.

One aim of this book is to reconcile the psychic and psychological aspects of the spiritual experience so that you can test the validity of this concept for yourself.

How can I contact my angel?

Although angels can appear to anyone, anywhere and at any time, if you want to contact them whenever you wish, you will need to raise your awareness of other levels of reality through meditation and visualisation exercises such as those described later in this book. Making contact in this way will help you to put the experience in context and allow you to test and interpret the impressions you receive.

How can I prove that the contact is genuine, not simply a product of my imagination?

The short answer is that it is quite simple to distinguish between the two, but it takes experience to avoid deceiving yourself. If an image arises spontaneously and cannot be manipulated at will then it is likely to be genuine. If you are going to pursue any form of psychic or spiritual self-exploration then you need to be aware that the lower self (the ego if you prefer) is likely to be highly selective when it comes to interpreting spiritual and psychic experiences for the purpose of self-aggrandisement. It may urge you to pursue past-life regression, for example, to discover that you were once Napoleon or Cleopatra, but you will have to be mature enough to accept the possibility that the truth is likely to be more mundane. There is more on this subject on pages 84–6.

You also have to remember that your conscious mind, or ego, is judgemental and will indulge in regrets and self-recrimination informing you of what you should have done in a certain situation and what you must do now. It is the voice of an overly critical parent but it can also be a cynical, self-indulgent teenager. In contrast, your guardian angel or higher self is loving and compassionate. It is forgiving, encouraging and gentle. Genuine communications from your guardian angel come through as a stream of consciousness, the words flowing faster than you can think. You will be genuinely touched and uplifted through your contact with the celestials.

How do I know if an angel is helping me if I can't see it?

You may have a sense of a presence in the room with you, you may see an archetypal figure or colours during a visualisation or you may feel an increasing warmth in your body when it is near you. But the most obvious evidence of angelic intervention is the increased number of coincidences that will occur in your life and the fact that problems will appear to solve themselves.

Why should I believe in angels if I have never seen one? And how can I appeal to them if I haven't had proof that they exist?

One of the aims of this book is to strengthen your belief in the existence of divine discarnate beings so that your appeals will carry conviction and the expectation that you will receive a response. It is unreasonable to expect anyone to believe in something out of the ordinary which they have not personally experienced, but if you follow the exercises in this book you will raise your awareness of angelic influence in your life and be able to validate the various experiences for yourself.

It is not necessary for you to envisage these beings as angels in the traditional sense. Many of the individuals who tell their own stories of angelic encounters in the following pages do not share the conventional idea of what angels might be. But they received help because they had faith in some form of benign presence which is concerned with our welfare and well-being.

In this secular age it is easy to underestimate the power of prayer and to feel self-conscious or cynical about asking for help from an unseen presence. But consider the case of US General George Patton, who was not too proud to appeal to God, in front of his staff, for four days of clear weather during a critical campaign in the final months of the Second World War. Within hours the clouds lifted and the allies were able to launch an air assault on the Germans which turned the tide of the war. The break in the weather lasted exactly four days before the snow clouds returned. Afterwards, Patton was not too proud to acknowledge the debt he owed to divine intervention in front of his hard-bitten officers.

What kind of things will they help me with?

Angels are not concerned exclusively with protecting you and your family. They can also assist in healing; improving relationships; helping you to find the right partner, a more fulfilling job or a new home and even inspiring you to be more creative. They can act as spiritual counsellors, resolving issues such as resentment, regret and guilt, and they can help to bring closure and comfort to the bereaved. Whenever you need guidance to make the right choice you can ask the advice of your angel as you would ask a best friend, guru or mentor.

Can I develop psychic powers with the aid of the angels?

Yes. In the process of opening yourself up to the angels you will also be increasing your awareness of other realities and attaining heightened states of consciousness. This acute sensitivity, or sixth sense, is the real meaning of the term 'psychic powers' and not the superhuman feats or phenomena depicted in fantasy fiction. In the course of this book I will show you how you can switch this state of heightened sensitivity on and off at will and I will describe the various abilities you can develop. These include seeing the aura (the etheric energy field around all living things, see pages 36–7), psychometry (picking up mental impressions from personal objects, see page 104) and recalling past-life experiences (see pages 84–6).

If angels exist, why do bad things happen to innocent people?

It is often difficult for us to understand why apparently innocent people have to suffer, but there could be a number of reasons. One is that these events force us to question the meaning and purpose of life and perhaps even stimulate us into improving the world rather than simply drifting aimlessly from day to day with no purpose other than self-gratification. For example, many advances in medicine, science, technology and human rights would not have occurred had we not been forced to find a solution to an existing problem or injustice. A tragic death can have the effect of arousing friends and family members to re-evaluate their own lives and search for meaning which they might not otherwise have done.

There is also the possibility that the parties involved in a violent incident or injustice may be resolving a karmic debt acquired in a previous life. Such explanations do not, of course, relieve us of the responsibility of coming to someone's assistance if we feel it is right, appropriate or necessary. But we should be aware that 'rescuing' someone in certain (non-violent) situations might not always be appropriate if they could have resolved the situation themselves. And, presumably, the angels operate on the same understanding. Life is a school in which we learn by example and experience. If the angels solved every problem for us, we wouldn't have to think for ourselves. How much would you have learnt, for example, if your parents had done your homework for you?

We have chosen to incarnate on the earth in order to exercise our free will and to determine our own destiny. The Chinese have a blessing which enforces this idea, 'May you be born in difficult times', the hope being that you will have an eventful life in which you will see every difficulty as a challenge and hence an opportunity to grow.

However, those who practise Kabbalah, the Jewish mystical tradition which is the foundation of the Western esoteric tradition and magic, believe that angels are confined to the upper worlds and are not permitted to intervene in human affairs under any circumstances. Kabbalists might argue that it is the individual's own higher self which manifests to bring comfort in times of despair and not a guardian angel, or that the two are one and the same. This is a point I hope to resolve during the course of this book.

Why do angels help some people and not others?

This follows on from the previous answer. If we knew that all our distress calls would be answered it is unlikely that we would make the decisions that we need to make in order to learn a particular lesson.

I believe that our guardian angel, or higher self, is continually inspiring and guiding us, but that we are often deaf to the quiet inner voice, or distracted or simply too wilful and eager to have our own way to pay it the attention it deserves. If we trusted what we commonly call our intuition, then we wouldn't find ourselves in conflict with others, or in unproductive relationships and unsatisfying jobs.

Do I need to ask a specific angel to help with a particular problem?

Some esoteric teachers might argue that appealing to a specific angel can be dangerous because it is a form of magic and that if we are psychologically unprepared we could be overwhelmed by the assimilation of angelic energy. However, I see no harm in appealing to angels if you regard them as personifications of the Divine and your intentions are for the highest good of all concerned. That said, I would still urge you to work through the exercises that appear later in this book to ensure that you are suitably grounded and centred. After all, you wouldn't think of exploring a foreign country without a smattering of basic phrases and a guidebook, so why not take equally practical precautions in your spiritual work?

If angels exist, could there also be demons?

No. It is my understanding that if there is a hierarchy of existence it is an extension of the natural world and conforms to the concept expressed in the ancient saying 'as above, so below'. In this scenario the less developed forms of life such as micro-organisms, insects and so on would be at the bottom, with humans at the mid-point and discarnate beings in the non-physical state, one stage removed from the divine source in the realm of pure consciousness. Such a progressive, ever-evolving universe does not allow for the existence of a contrary negative force.

If you believe that the universe is the expression of a loving God, how could it be possible for the Divine to manifest something contrary to its own nature? Surely that which is perfect cannot create something which is imperfect.

If I open myself to angelic influence, is there a danger that I might contact something evil?

It is my understanding that evil does not exist as a separate conscious entity. Only certain people and their destructive acts could be described as evil. Evil is the denial of our divine nature expressed as a lack of empathy for our fellow creatures. There is overwhelming evidence of the existence of angels from the earliest times to the present day, but no one of sound mind has ever claimed to have seen a demon. Demons and devils are a creation of the unenlightened mind, which exists in a world of fear and suspicion of its own making.

My experience – and that of the many psychics and healers with whom I have worked for almost twenty years – is that there is nothing to fear 'out there'. Only very rarely do experienced psychics who practise what is known as 'soul rescuing' come into contact with a restless, troubled soul who is drawn to a like-minded individual with whom it can re-experience whatever form of violence, or abusive behaviour or substance it was addicted to in life.

So long as you follow the instructions in this book for attaining an altered state of consciousness safely and avoid irresponsible practices which involve seeking power over other people or dabbling with Ouija boards, you will be safe. If you seek contact with the angels with good intentions and for a positive purpose such as healing, obtaining guidance or increasing self-awareness, then you are unlikely to have any unpleasant experiences. But remember: at all times you are in control.

2

My Personal
Experience of
Angels

I have been teaching meditation and psychic development for more than fifteen years, but I must confess that I was not consciously aware of the presence or influence of the angels in my life until I began holding angel workshops in the mid 1990s.

As I child I had out-of-body experiences which convinced me that we are more than merely physical beings and that there is a greater reality beyond this physical dimension. But I still believed that coincidence, luck, fate and free will played their part in defining our lives (the latter two are not as mutually exclusive as you might think).

Then at the end of 1990 I ended a frustrating relationship and despaired of finding someone with whom I could settle down and have a family. So I asked the angels to send me the partner who was right for me, regardless of whether she conformed to my ideal or not. I gave the problem over to the angels and got on with my life, which was then centred on song writing and music journalism. Exactly a year to the day later my wife-to-be knocked on my front door with a view to interviewing me for a radio station about the albums that I had released. She had flown from her home in Germany to England 'on a hunch' having seen my photograph and felt that we might have 'a connection'. At the time I had not written any books so she wasn't aware of my interest in mysticism. She didn't know my personal circumstances. I could have been married already for all she knew and, of course, it's possible that I might not have been at home on that particular day.

A year later we were married and we now have two children. Incidentally, she shares my interest in mysticism and my spiritual philosophy, which is a rare thing and of enormous practical help to me as a teacher and writer. Most of the psychics and healers that I work with have a constant struggle against their partner's scepticism.

You would think that such an experience would have convinced me that angels exist, but no. I still maintained that we are the centre of our own universe and that my wife and I had made an unconscious connection. The universe does not, however, allow us to remain unenlightened for long.

Invisible friends

After the birth of our first son, Michael, I was asked to hold a workshop on the subject of 'how to contact your guardian angel' which I accepted, although I had misgivings as I had not yet seen an angel myself. A few days later I went outside to look at the stars, when the idea came to me to ask for angelic protection for the house. The next moment there appeared a transparent figure as high as the house, with a sword in its grasp. It had a serious, intimidating expression, not at all as I had imagined an angel to look. I didn't have a sense of its presence and it didn't acknowledge me, which suggests that I had a glimpse of something existing in another reality rather than something which had been invoked into our world. After a few moments it faded from view. It was not solid and it didn't radiate an aura of compassion as did the angels that other people have described, but it certainly fitted the bill for an angel you would want guarding your home if you could summon one up at will.

Even this experience did not convince me entirely. I pride myself on having a more psychological approach in which to contextualise spiritual and psychic experiences, and prefer to believe that most phenomena result from awakening our own unlimited potential as divine beings rather than from the influence of invisible forces. But then shortly afterwards my two-year-old son Michael kept referring to an invisible friend of his called 'Malakha'. At first I thought he had adapted his own name, but then in the course of research for another book I came upon the Hebrew word 'Malakh' (pronounced 'Malakha'), which means messenger or angel. After that Michael didn't mention Malakha again. I can only assume it was because the message had been received.

The workshop went well. We had 70 people on the first night, with some travelling 50 miles (80 kilometres) or more to be there. To my surprise more than half of the class comprised young people in their late teens and twenties and several had had quite extraordinary experiences. A lady who had never even meditated before described becoming detached from her body then lifted into a heightened state of awareness, at which point she began to feel anxious and uneasy, never having experienced anything like it before. She then described seeing the spirit of two of her deceased relatives who reassured her that everything would be all right.

They helped her return safely and with the knowledge that no one really dies. Others talked of seeing vibrant colours, feeling heat or sensing a presence.

More remarkable in its way was the time I taught meditation evening classes at an adult education centre. One night three of my students made contact with their deceased fathers during a visualisation that had made no mention of spirits. In fact, the rules of the centre dictated that I had to remove all reference to spiritual matters to conform to the course description as 'meditation for stress relief and relaxation'. For that reason I removed all reference to an angel in a subsequent meditation and yet one lady came out of the visualisation exhilarated by the experience and claiming that she had just met an angel!

Angelic literary agents!

Although I had seen an angel, I did not need to have the evidence of my own eyes to believe that angels exist. I believe in them because I sense their presence on an almost daily basis and I have all the proof I need that they have helped me whenever I asked for their assistance.

When I am writing on spiritual and psychic subjects I often feel an invisible hand ruffling my hair, caressing my ear or occasionally even prodding me in the chest as if to let me know that they are around and that I am on the right track. I have also felt invisible hands under my own when giving healing, which sounds unnerving but in the context was calming and reassuring.

But the real proof, as far as I am concerned, is in the frequent occasions when I have received practical help when I needed it most. I have mentioned the circumstances under which I met my wife, but after that there were numerous incidents when we were helped out of difficulties by angelic intervention.

One particularly memorable incident occurred in January 1998 when several music magazines that I had been writing for ceased publication. My wife was looking after our first child full-time, so we were entirely dependent on my income. As the overdraft limit loomed I asked the angels specifically for book work as reviewing was obviously too precarious under the circumstances. Within a week a major publisher invited me to its London office to discuss various projects, the first of which I hadn't actually suggested!

What I learnt from that experience was that the angels will only help if you ask them and that you have to be prepared to accept what they give you. In this case I took on a subject with which I was not familiar, but I saw it as an opportunity provided by the angels for me to learn and develop as a writer.

Six years later I had a dozen books to my credit but I was frustrated that they were not being promoted. So again, I appealed to the angels and within a month the publisher changed its policy and hired an independent public relations company who organised several interviews and secured a double-page feature in a national newspaper for my latest book.

A lesson learnt

But perhaps the most convincing evidence of the angels' willingness to intervene occurred in October 2003 when I was experiencing another of my occasional lean periods. My wife was also frustrated in her ambitions at the time, being stuck in a low-paid, dead-end job with no prospects of promotion. This time we didn't hesitate to call on the angels. We combined our efforts and affirmed that we were willing to accept whatever they provided.

Shortly afterwards my wife reluctantly attended an interview with a local employment agency, convinced that there couldn't possibly be anything suitable for her in the area. She returned with the offer of a job with a company that she hadn't been aware of and which had only been registered with the agency that morning. Taking the hint, I offered to give up my writing career (which appeared to have come to a natural dead end) and accept anything for which I was qualified. I accepted a part-time job helping disabled students to find work experience placements and was due to start on the following Monday. However, on the Friday before, I received a commission for three magazine articles that I hadn't been expecting and the next day a royalty cheque from a publisher that, again, I hadn't been expecting. The Germans have an expression for such events. They call it a 'Wink mit dem Zaunpfahl', which roughly translates as 'a hint with a fence stick': a heavy-handed hint.

Sometimes it is not enough to ask for help from the angels and expect assistance; we have to demonstrate by our actions and attitude that we acknowledge that higher forces have our best interests at heart and that we are willing to submit to their influence. I had been taking my privileged life for granted to some extent and needed to be woken up to the fact that there are many people who are not so fortunate. Having learnt the lesson, I was allowed to continue with my career.

Psychologists might argue that such events were instigated by a change in my attitude and the happy coincidences they call synchronicity. But neither explains the good fortune that befell an elderly relative of mine who asked her guardian angel for the means to pay for the landscaping of her large and rambling garden because it was proving too much for her to maintain. That same day the phone company called to offer compensation for having mistakenly charged her for two lines instead of one for more than twenty years. The refund was precisely the amount she needed to pay for the landscaping.

Experience has taught me that you do not have to subscribe to a specific religion or philosophy in order to appeal for help from the angels. As a divine being you have the right to ask for their assistance and to expect their help so long as you acknowledge their assistance and thank them accordingly. After all, nobody likes being taken for granted!

It continually amazes me that we readily open ourselves to so many negative influences and believe whatever we read or hear in the media and yet we hesitate to call on the universal life force which sustains us and exists for our well-being. It is perhaps understandable that in this digital age many people are reluctant to believe in the existence of angels, but the evidence is overwhelming.

In the course of this book I will outline various techniques to help you become more aware of the angelic influence in your life and ensure that your requests are answered as promptly and effectively as those I have described.

Note: In accordance with esoteric tradition I am obliged to point out that this book is my personal interpretation of the invisible realms and its inhabitants as passed down to me by my teachers and filtered through revelation and personal experience. Each reader should weigh the truth of what follows for themselves and accept only what feels right for them.

3

Angelic Encounters

'The world of spirit is not closed, your consciousness is closed...' Goethe

When a notorious criminal approached 'Blessed Breet', a Dutch lay preacher, and asked for a word in private, Breet expected to be threatened with violence. His missionary work was having a detrimental effect on business in the town's red light district and the streets were rife with the rumour that he was to be persuaded to take the 'good news' elsewhere. But to the preacher's surprise the man made a confession which Breet was to later to record in his memoirs.

The stranger was eager to unburden himself of a guilty secret and find absolution before he died, a fact which convinced Breet that the man's story was true.

It appeared that twenty years earlier, in the early 1900s, he and another man had plotted to kill the preacher by luring him to a quiet area of the town and drowning him in the canal. But they had abandoned their plan when they saw the preacher walking with two companions. Breet was able to recall the night in question after the criminal mentioned that they had tricked him into coming to a particular street on a false errand.

'I remember that night,' answered Breet. 'But I was on my own.'

'No,' said the repentant murderer. 'My friend and I clearly saw someone on each side of you.'

'Then the Lord must have sent two angels to keep me safe,' concluded Breet with satisfaction.

The popular image of an angel as a heavenly human being with wings and a halo is at odds with the descriptions given by those who claim to have actually seen one, many of whom did not believe in the existence of angels prior to their experience.

A typical example was the following incident, which was related to Dutch doctor H.C. Moolenburgh in the 1980s by one of his patients.

When his patient was a little girl her mother visited a child who was seriously ill. As she prayed with the child's mother a young man appeared and asked what was wrong. On being told that a child was dying the young man went to the child's room, laid his hands gently on her and cast out the illness with prayer. Then without a word, he left and was never seen again. No one in the village had seen him come or go and no one living in the surrounding area fitted his description. The child awoke from her coma as soon as the stranger left and the next day was indignant that she was not allowed to go to school.

Dr Moolenburgh was so impressed that he subsequently made a study of the subject, conducting a survey of 400 patients during which he collected numerous first-hand accounts which were later published. But it was not only his patients who had moving stories to tell. One of his friends was in fear for his life when an angel appeared, having apparently walked through a closed window. The friend described the angel as having a nebulous, luminous appearance which prompted him to remark that he now understood why angels are depicted with wings. 'It is their radiance', he concluded. The apparition offered a few comforting words and disappeared. And with that, the crisis passed.

Anecdotal evidence

During my research for this book I solicited friends, family and colleagues for memories of their angelic encounters and received the following which shed light on the nature of angels and the many ways in which they can interact with us.

Health and lifestyle journalist Jo Malby describes her first angelic encounter back in 1999.

'I had just moved in to my new flat and felt strangely uncomfortable. It was very old and unfamiliar after my previous cramped but cosy studio apartment. To make matters worse, I had broken five ligaments the day before and was in a lot of pain. It was so bad that I couldn't sit in a chair. I had to lie on the floor. All I could do was rest and stare at the ceiling. Due to the pain and the boredom I guess I must have drifted into an altered state of consciousness because I then sensed a presence in the room. I didn't know exactly what it was at first. I was expecting spirit activity I suppose, the ghost of the previous tenant perhaps. But I just didn't want to look. Then it was as if someone ever so gently turned my head for me to look at the corner where the wall meets the high ceiling.

'As I did, tiny shards of light were beaming towards me from this incredibly bright centre – it was like nothing I'd ever seen or experienced before. I was no longer frightened, simply in awe. As the light penetrated my being, I felt what can only be described as pure love. The pain in my ankle subsided as if it was now surrounded by some kind of etheric cotton wool. I was being hugged from the inside and out – the feeling was simply phenomenal. I must have fallen asleep after that because when I looked at the clock seven hours had passed, although it had only felt like two minutes. It left me feeling incredibly refreshed and alive.

'After this experience, there were many coincidences. Having just moved into the flat, nobody had my address, but there would be post in the morning addressed to me, with details of angel workshops. I was then asked to write an article on angels for a website shortly before meeting many people who had also been touched by these beyond-beautiful beings.

'I know my angel is always with me, I feel guided and protected since that first experience and I know that I can do anything and go anywhere with her.'

Spiritual Samaritans

Some people might dismiss such experiences as the product of an overactive imagination, but even the most hardened cynic would find it difficult to explain some of the extraordinary things which have happened to apparently 'ordinary' people. Take for example the case of ex-Ministry of Defence fireman John Claret, who prides himself on being pragmatic and not given to flights of fancy.

During the late 1990s John and his family were driving through the countryside when they found themselves stuck behind a slow-moving car. When they came to a straight stretch of road with good visibility John decided to overtake. There was a lorry approaching some distance away, but there appeared to be plenty of time to pass the car in front. Just as John was pulling out he had an overwhelming feeling of fear that instinctively caused him to pull back behind the car. As he did so a sports car pulled out from behind the lorry at high speed. John is convinced that if he had not pulled back in time he would have struck it head on. The incident convinced him that he and his family were saved by his guardian angel.

On another occasion John left home on the Kent coast early one Sunday morning by car to attend an important meeting at Battersea Town Hall.

'I had no idea where it was,' he recalls, 'but I thought I could ask when I got into London. I left home with a feeling of calm and trust that everything would be all right so I wasn't worried. I must have sensed that I would get help in some form. Driving along the dual carriageway before I joined the motorway I spotted a young man thumbing a lift. He looked respectable so I pulled over and asked how far he was going. He told me he wanted to get back home to London. And when I told him that I was going there he asked if I could drop him off at Battersea as that was where he lived.

'I was amazed as this was about 70 miles (113 kilometres) away and he was going to the same place as me. He said he would show me the town hall because he actually lived right behind it. When we arrived he got out while I parked the car, but when I looked around to thank him, he was gone.

'If he hadn't helped me I would never have found it in time as there was no one around at that time in the morning to ask directions. Looking back on it, I'm convinced that he was either an angel in human form or that angelic influence had placed him in the right place at the right time.'

Thousands of similar stories go unrecorded every day, usually because the person concerned feels that what they have experienced was a gift from God. It is their own private miracle which is to be treasured and not demeaned by being exposed to public speculation and maybe even ridicule. On many occasions I have been interviewed by sceptical radio presenters who evidently felt obliged to question the existence of psychic phenomena to appease their listeners. But after giving me the chance to present my case, several have admitted on air that they have been saved from physical harm by an unseen hand which they attributed to their guardian angel. I suspect that given the right setting and a sympathetic hearing many people would admit to having had similar experiences, but society sneers at the miraculous because we are afraid of questioning what we perceive as reality. Occasionally, however, someone will be so profoundly affected by the miracle they have witnessed that they feel compelled to tell the world about it, regardless of the consequences.

Journalist Lydia Prince described such an incident in her account of the 1929 Arab uprising, 'Appointment In Jerusalem'. Lydia was a forerunner of the intrepid female news reporter whom we now regularly see reporting from a war zone on the nightly TV news. But in the 1920s she was one of a kind.

Bridge over Chaos by John Martin

During the conflict she rescued an abandoned baby and took refuge in a house surrounded by both Arab and Jewish fighters. As the bullets and shells ricocheted around her she feared for the infant's safety. If she remained in the house the baby would die of thirst, as the water supply had been cut off. But if she took her chances outside, she was certain to be caught in the crossfire.

Desperate, she offered a prayer for divine protection and in the next moment there was silence. Not a shot was fired. Cautiously, she stepped outside, with the infant cradled in her arms, and hurried through the rubble-strewn streets. Eventually she came to a barricade that was too high to scramble over and in despair she sat down, uncertain what to do next. At that critical moment a youth appeared dressed in Western clothes and took the child from her. He said nothing as he helped Lydia over the barricade and through a labyrinth of deserted streets which had been the scene of a fierce gun battle only minutes before. Eventually he came to a house out of range of the fighting that was certain to resume any second and there he passed the baby back to Lydia. He left without speaking and before the exhausted journalist could thank him. When he had gone Lydia took a closer look at her surroundings and recognised the house as the home of a friend, who took her in and helped her look after the baby. When Lydia described her rescuer the friend was puzzled. She knew nobody fitting that description and the pair were left to conclude that Lydia's prayer had been answered in the most practical way.

Angels of comfort and consolation

Although there are numerous credible accounts of people being plucked from impending danger by unseen hands, the most common form of angelic visitation is one which brings comfort to the despairing and the bereaved. The presence of these beings is usually accompanied by a tangible sense of unconditional love and compassion, which can make even the most rational person emotional when recalling the incident.

British actor William Roach, who is known to millions of TV viewers as Ken Barlow in the long-running soap opera *Coronation Street*, suffered the death of his eighteen-month-old daughter Edwina and later described the grief as being so great that it was almost a physical pain. For several days William and his wife could neither eat nor sleep. He found it difficult to leave the house and he broke down whenever he tried to have a conversation on the telephone. Then on the morning of the funeral he experienced something which eased his suffering and profoundly affected his understanding of life and death.

'I woke up and there was this glowing – I call it a glory – a round glowing light and in the middle was Edwina's little face smiling. At the same time as seeing this – and I saw it, there was no question, it wasn't a dream or anything – came this great feeling of love. And the grief lifted. It didn't go entirely, but it lifted to quite a large extent.'

Then William's wife woke up and remarked that she felt better, which prompted him to tell her what he had just seen. From that moment on, he says that their grief changed to a feeling of almost enjoyment at having had the pleasure of that child for those eighteen months.

'When she appeared in this sort of glowing glory I knew that there was an angelic being that was helping her to appear like that.

'Belief is a very feeble word,' he concludes. 'I know of the existence of angels. I've seen that angelic materialisation through Edwina. I feel it all the time. That has helped me to an understanding and I don't need any further proof of it. I know of their presence. I feel their presence and I'm aware of the help they give.'

Another incident involved Richard O'Brien, creator of the cult musical *The Rocky Horror Picture Show*.

Richard was alone in his flat suffering severe depression after the failure of his marriage when he felt two strong invisible arms grasp him from behind and embrace him with such a sense of unconditional love and reassurance that he was moved to tears. However, later that day he began to doubt that such a thing could have occurred. It then happened again, as if to confirm that he had not imagined it. Again he was moved to tears by the overwhelming sense of unconditional love emanating from his unseen angel whose message appeared to be that we are never truly alone nor does our suffering go unseen.

The library angel

One of the most curious examples of angelic intervention is the phenomenon known as the 'library angel'. In these cases someone unexpectedly comes across a particular book for which they have been searching under circumstances which challenge their belief in mere coincidence. One of the most celebrated cases occurred when the actor Sir Anthony Hopkins discovered an abandoned copy of a book he had been searching for lying in plain sight on a bench at an underground station on his way home. He later discovered that it was the very copy that had been lost by a friend of his.

The novelist Dame Rebecca West had an equally remarkable experience while searching for a particular volume on the Nuremberg Trials at the Royal Institute of International Affairs. In an attempt to prove to the librarian that their cataloguing system was a shambles, she pulled out a book at random and discovered that she had chosen the volume that she had been looking for. Moreover, it had fallen open at the precise page she needed.

<u>4</u>

The Angel
Experience

For the past fifteen years during my work as a spiritual teacher and counsellor I have had the pleasure of working with a number of very gifted psychics and healers. During the course of writing this book I took the opportunity of interviewing those who acknowledge the assistance of angels in their spiritual work to see if their experiences would shed a new light on the nature and purpose of these celestial beings.

The guiding light of angels

Karin Page, founder of the Star of the East spiritual healing centre in Kent, has experienced angels in all their forms – as an unseen presence, as a vision in meditation, as an answer to prayer and, that rarest of all encounters, the angel who manifests in physical form.

'When I was a young woman in Malaya I was returning from an outing with some friends when the driver of our car lost control. The car went down an embankment and stopped with its back wheels hanging over a ledge with a long drop into a flooded quarry. The other passengers managed to scramble out on the roadside leaving me and the driver petrified with fear and unable to move in case the movement sent the car over the edge. Despite my fear, for some reason I sat perfectly calm and didn't say a word. Just then a young man appeared, calmed the other passengers and gestured for them to come back to the car and pull it to safety. Then he disappeared back into the jungle without saying a word. Once we were free the driver told me that if I had screamed he would have panicked and tried to climb out the passenger side, which would certainly have tipped the car over the edge. But because I had seemed so calm and certain of rescue he sat still. Even now I can't believe that I didn't scream.'

Karin is not always so placid and patient when dealing with the angels.

'Sometimes you have to let them know how important or urgent your problem is in the most direct terms possible. My granddaughter had been waiting more than two years for a kidney donor, as no one in the family was a suitable match, when I lost patience one day, stormed into my healing sanctuary and yelled at the top of my voice to the angels, berating them for not helping. Within a couple of days a donor had been found and my granddaughter's life had been saved.'

At other times the angels make their presence known in more subtle ways.

'I often have a vision of an angel in meditation, particularly when I'm sitting in circle with a group. The presence of other people seems to raise the energy level and make contact more likely. One of the most memorable experiences happened when we were led in a guided visualisation into an imagined landscape. We were told to visualise a path leading to two doors, one of which was marked "healing" and the other "knowledge". I chose to go through the healing door because I had just been diagnosed with diabetes and was feeling low. I found myself in a dark room with a high ceiling and then a silvery white, shimmering, misty apparition appeared which lit up the whole room. It was a beautiful angel with an exquisite face. It filled the room from floor to ceiling but the curious thing was that the corners of the room remained in shadow and that is something that wouldn't have happened if it had been a product of my imagination. Then I heard it say, "Sit down and receive a de-light-ful healing," with the emphasis on "light". I felt as if I was floating and long after I had come out of the meditation I still felt that detachment and sense of peace. I have had similar experiences in the past, but this was different. The energy I felt was quite cool, soothing and calming.

'I don't need to know who the angels are and I don't require proof that they exist. I think that the message is what is important, not the messenger.'

Sometimes the message comes in the form of an inner voice which Karin has learnt to trust without question.

'When I was a child my parents brought me to Ramsgate in Kent for a holiday and one day while playing on the beach I heard a voice say, "When you are older you will return here and this is where you will do your life's work." Years later the prophecy came true. I moved to Ramsgate and began to look for a building where I could start a healing sanctuary. One day I was considering an old Masonic Lodge which was in a terrible state of disrepair. My husband who was a practical man warned me not to take it as it would cost thousands of pounds to make it habitable. Then I heard that reassuring inner voice again. This time it instructed me to go outside and look at the entrance. I went out and there I saw an inscription above the door, "Lodge Number X The Star of the East". That was the deciding factor because a year earlier a medium had described my spirit guide as an Indian woman wearing a talisman that she called "the Star of the East".

And for years people had been giving me presents with stars on the wrapping paper or as some prominent feature of the present. I knew then that I had found the right place and when I was offered a seven or fourteen year lease I immediately took the longer commitment. And since that day I have never looked back, as the centre has attracted dozens of spiritual teachers and provided healing to hundreds of people from all over this part of Kent.'

Recently Karen's unshakeable belief in the existence of angels appeared to receive confirmation from an unexpected source.

'A respected scientist called Harry Oldfield invited a friend and me to test a new technique for photographing the aura, the human energy field which is invisible to the eye but can be seen by psychics. Oldfield had devised a way of linking a conventional camera to a computer program to capture energy at a particular frequency beyond the range of conventional cameras, in a similar way to X-rays, which he called Aura Imaging. When he photographed me he got the shock of his life. Around my shoulders you could clearly see the radiance of what looked like wings formed by the aura. "I'm no angel," I said, but it was there on film and my friend witnessed it. But what convinced me that it wasn't a trick of the light was the fact that I had severe laryngitis that day and could hardly speak. In the photograph over my throat was a bright red spot.' (See 'Exercise: Auric wings', page 68.)

Artistic angels

We tend to think of angels as celestial Samaritans, but there is reason to believe that they can also inspire us to be creative. Psychic artist Sylvia Gainsford (illustrator of the *Tarot of the Old Path* and my own Kabbalah cards) has experienced the guiding hand of the angels on many occasions while working in her studio in Wales.

'Normally, when painting landscapes or portraits I have to consider carefully which colours I am going to use and I have to test them on paper before applying them to the picture. But when I am illustrating a set of tarot cards the pictures seem to paint themselves without any conscious effort on my part. The same happened when I illustrated the Kabbalah cards. I am normally very particular about the tone of the colours and I judge every detail minutely before committing myself on paper, but when painting the cards I found that I was mixing colour almost without looking, as if guided by an unseen hand.

'I feel the presence of the angels rather than see them. Personally, I don't need to see them to know that they are there inspiring me. When they are with me the atmosphere is charged with a distinctive energy and I can work at great speed and for a long time without rest. When illustrating

Tiferet, Sylvia Gainsford's illustration for my Kabbalah cards

the *Tarot of the Old Path* I would work all day and on into the early hours of the morning, day after day. Normally that relentless routine would have exhausted me, but when the angels are with me I feel exhilarated. It was like painting with my eyes closed through the entire project.

'When I draw them I depict them in human form with wings because I think that is symbolic. I don't think they really look like that. They are a form of energy beyond our comprehension, but by using the traditional form, people from all over the world can link in and be assured that there is something beyond this limited physical dimension.'

In addition to illustrating tarot cards, Sylvia also gives readings to visitors to her gallery in Wales.

'I have sensed the presence of the angels many times during readings. They always seem to come as I tune in to the client just after shuffling the cards and prior to laying them out. It is as if they appear in order to act as a link between us. Sometimes I will have a vision of the spirit in my mind and sense its personality but I don't get a distinct face. It's like when someone sits next to you in a bus or train and without looking at them you get a feeling about them. They emanate a quality of energy that you can pick up on if you are sensitive and you just know that they are in a bad mood, or whatever.'

Sylvia's experience of angels goes beyond mere guidance. She recalls an incident in which her guardian angel intervened to save her from certain danger.

'I remember the details of that night and the sense of the angel's presence as if it were only days and not years ago, which I believe is a characteristic of angelic encounters. As I recall it now I can feel the strange sensation again, as if I am reconnecting with that spirit.

'During the 1960s I was a teenager living in Tunbridge Wells and one evening I was returning home when I found myself immersed in a thick fog. I could only see a very short distance in front of me, but I knew the area well and so I wasn't too worried. But then I turned down a narrow lane and a few moments later I heard shouting and the sound of breaking glass coming from the other end. It sounded like a large group of drunken youths and that made me very nervous indeed. I couldn't go back and they were approaching fast so I groped my way along the wall to my left until I found a gate which led to the allotments. Unfortunately, I was on a gravel path and if I had moved the drunks would have heard me. Just at that moment as the panic rose in me I sensed a presence standing behind me. I instinctively reached back to acknowledge it, thinking that it must be a friend of mine – I know that sounds odd and illogical, but at the time I had the strongest feeling that I knew who it was. The panic feeling left me in an instant and the drunks passed by without seeing me. When they had gone I turned to thank my "friend" and of course there was nobody there. So, to me an angel is not a projection of our own unconscious or higher self, but a distinct individual energy – at least that one was.

'I see the angels as spirit beings which have a direct link with the Divine. From my experience I can't see them arranged in a hierarchy with designated powers and jobs to do. Categorising angels in that way is like spiritual trainspotting. It's nonsense and thinking of them in human terms only serves to confuse and block your access to them.'

Sylvia's advice to those who want to strengthen their connection with the angels is to keep it simple.

'I don't feel the need for any complicated ritual. If you learn to trust your intuition it won't lead you astray and you will strengthen your connection with your guardian angel.

'Another way is to go out at night and simply look up at the stars. Lose your sense of self in the vast emptiness of space and accept that there is so much that is unknown to you. We are all so self-centred, so becoming one with the Universe in this way can bring about a powerful contact with the angels.

'My experience of the angels has given me a tremendous feeling of not being alone and a wonderful comforting feeling that we all have spiritual back-up whenever we need it.'

Angels on the other side

Kent psychic Jill Nash has a slightly different perspective on the nature of angels gleaned from more than forty years' experience as a medium.

'I have come to the conclusion that an angel is any form of spirit guide and it muddies the connection if you try to impose a specific name and job description on the discarnate being that is helping you.

'If you have to define what angels and guides do then I would say that from my experience spirit guides seem to work with us on specific problems at different times in our lives, whereas angels are around us all the time and respond to our emotions. I believe that we all have our own personal angel who is with us from the moment we are born, who we can sense if we meditate and attune to their higher vibration.'

Jill's belief in angels is bolstered by her own personal encounter with a celestial being when she was sitting in a meditation circle many years ago with a small group of like-minded mediums.

'We must have tuned into that particular vibrational frequency on which the angels exist because at one point we all automatically linked hands without saying anything to each other. The next moment this beautiful golden light appeared in the centre of the circle and although it was intensely bright it didn't hurt our eyes. We could look right into it. We couldn't make out a face or tell if it was a man or a woman, but it was definitely in a human form. It was a beautiful being about six or seven feet (two metres) tall and radiating such love that we all had tears streaming down our faces. It only lasted a few seconds, but it brought such an energy with it that I'll never ever forget it. I like to think that it appeared as a sign to reassure us that we were on the right path.'

Such experiences might sound remarkable to those who are new to such phenomena, but psychics, or 'sensitives' as many prefer to be called, are constantly aware of the existence of other realities.

'I have always known that there is another world which co-exists with our own. It's not up there in Heaven or down there. It is all around us. And the sooner we realise that nothing actually dies then we will lose our fear of the unknown and be more open to this greater reality. We all have the gift of clairvoyance, of seeing beyond the physical dimension, but our perception is dulled by the rational side of the brain which dismisses these subtle impressions as figments of the imagination. There is a lot of truth in that old saying, "For those who believe no proof is necessary and for those who do not believe, no proof is possible."'

Although Jill understands why some people feel the need to make a special ritual in preparation for communicating with the angels, her personal approach is to keep it simple.

'I must admit all I do is sit quietly, clear my mind of everyday concerns and light a candle to attract the angels. I've worked as a medium at Stanstead Hall, the so-called "psychic school" in Essex where some of the best known psychics work and teach, and they have told me the importance of opening up and closing down, but I don't feel the need for that. I sometimes see spirits walk in with the person who has come to me for a reading and I describe them in detail to the astonishment of the living partner who confirms all that I have said about their appearance and personality. I'm open all the time. I don't feel the need for a special ritual. I've given readings at psychic fayres where the other mediums unpack whole suitcases full of spiritual paraphernalia such as crystal balls, tarot cards and so on. Then they stare at me in disbelief sitting behind a bare table without even a cloth to cover it and wonder how I can function without all the accessories, but to me psychic sensitivity is perfectly natural. It is not something you try hard to attain, it's something that you relax into.'

Jill believes that the most effective way to establish a strong connection with the angels is to make a habit of communicating with them on a regular basis and acting on the understanding that they are around you all the time.

'I talk to them every day either in my head or sometimes even out loud when no one else is about! If I have a decision to make I'll pick up a suitable book and ask them to guide me to a page that will give me the answer. Then I'll open the book at random and invariably find the answer. At other times I'll tell them my problem and give it over to them to solve, then some time later the solution will just pop into my head.

'On occasion they will help in practical ways. For example, recently a friend of mine was in great distress because her central heating boiler had expired and she had been told it would cost £1000 to replace it. She didn't have the money and was worried that she would have no heating and no hot water. I reassured her that the angels always help those in genuine need. I told her that I had received a message from Spirit [the angels] the day before telling me that she was going to have some difficulty but that the problem was being taken care of and that she wasn't to worry. A few days later she phoned me to tell me that she had just received a cheque for £2000. Her brother had cashed in some bonds left by their mother which had matured that month and sent it to her, not knowing that she had been desperate for the money!'

What would she say to those people who have asked the angels for help but didn't receive it?

'I think that they have to accept that sometimes it isn't the right time for the angels to intervene. Sometimes we have to struggle to find a solution because we have to learn something from that situation. If we could call on the angels for every little problem that we had then we would delegate responsibility for our lives to the higher beings and we would never grow and evolve, which is the purpose of our incarnation on the Earth. Life is not a holiday camp, it's an opportunity for learning through experience and not all experience is pleasant.

'We have to understand that everything the angels do is done out of love and even the most loving parents know that they have to let their children learn from their own mistakes. I think that is the key to explaining our relationship with the angels.'

Angels in Arizona

Occult expert and author Howard Rodway, creator of the best-selling *Tarot of the Old Path*, has given the subject a great deal of thought and has his own idea as to what angels might be.

'I was brought up in a strict Christian school where religion was rammed down our throats on a daily basis and yet my mother was a witch. She was a wonderful woman who taught me about the healing power of herbs and made me aware of the power we all have within us. So I don't subscribe to the Christian concept of angels as divine messengers in human form with wings and a halo. My many psychic experiences have led me to consider angels as being a generic term for all forms of spirit guides.'

Howard had two very memorable experiences which he believes illustrate different aspects of the angel experience.

'The first occurred in 1979 when I was travelling through Arizona on a Greyhound bus. We were pulling into a small rest stop called Huock when my attention was caught by two young Navajo men who were wearing identical red shirts and blue jeans. They were sitting on a fence by the side of the road and staring right at me. As I looked, I heard them say in unison, "You are all strangers passing through. One day this land will return to us. Assuming that, we have the patience to wait."

'The odd thing was that the window was closed and they were too far away from the bus for me to have heard them as clearly as I did. But their voices were as distinct as if we had been having a conversation in the street and I remember their exact words to this day. When we got off the bus I mentioned the incident to one of the elders at the restaurant and he didn't seem surprised at all. He told me that the two young men were what they call "the deer people" and that they were shape-shifters.

'The fact that people all over the world share a belief in spirit guides in some form while the traditional image of winged deities is confined to the Judeo-Christian and Islamic religion suggests that angels appear in a form which we can accept. Their true form will not be known to us until we are on the other side of life.'

Howard's second angelic experience led him to conclude that our guardian angel might not be an external entity, but rather an aspect of our higher self.

'Many years ago I had a dream in which I found myself in an exotic location which I took to be somewhere in North Africa. In the dream I was lost. All I could see was a mosque above a ravine. Just then a disembodied voice said, "If you keep the mosque in sight you will find the Arab's home." It seemed significant at that moment, but when I woke up it made no sense at all. I mentioned it to my wife because it had seemed so real and it was in colour. I thought that was very curious.

'Some months later our travel agent phoned to say that the holiday destination we wanted was unavailable and that all they had left for that week was Morocco. So we went. In Marakesh we met a guide who invited us for a meal at his home. Afterwards he asked us to visit him again before we left to say goodbye. On that last evening we got lost trying to find his apartment and then I saw the same mosque above the ravine that I had seen in my dream. The curious thing was that in the dream the mosque was finished but in Marakesh it was still being built. But it was definitely the same building and in the same location. We had nothing to lose so we followed the directions I had been given in the dream and we found our friend's apartment.

'Now the question is, whose voice was it in the dream – my higher self or my guardian angel? The fact that the voice came from within my own head suggests that they could be one and the same. But I heard the voices of the Navajo shape-shifters in my head. And why did I have that particular dream when it was not regarding a significant event in my life?'

Howard urges us to stop thinking of angels in conventional Judeo-Christian terms and consider them instead as agents of change who influence our lives in subtle ways.

'I am convinced that they put like-minded people in touch with each other for their mutual benefit. For example, many years ago I was working on a switchboard in a government establishment when I received a call from an American official working in the same building enquiring if I could recommend a good psychic medium. Usually we were asked for the name of a good local dentist or a theatre ticket agency, but he wanted a medium because his wife wanted a reading. He was evidently happy with the person I recommended because afterwards he phoned to thank me and take a note of my name and number. Then many years later his son came over from the States to make a documentary on the occult and called me to arrange a filmed interview about the tarot pack that I had just created. If I hadn't taken that call that night his mother wouldn't have received the message she needed to hear and I wouldn't have been rewarded with that interview years later. That is way the angels often work.

'Other times they work through us, giving us inspiration if we are open to it and helping us to express ideas. I have often written books in which the words flowed without me having to think about them consciously. I frequently look back at certain passages and sometimes even whole chapters and wonder how I wrote that.'

In the presence of angels

Derbyshire healer Pamela Redwood believes that angels appear at a particular point in an individual's development to raise their awareness of other realities, after which they withdraw to enable that person to determine their own destiny.

'For many years I saw angels as huge beings of light with enormous wings because I needed to have visual confirmation that I was on the right path and to give me the confidence that I needed to offer healing to people. Knowing that I was working with the angels made me feel less self-conscious. But as I became more certain of my own abilities I saw them less often in that idealised form and began to perceive them as coloured spheres of energy. Now I don't need to see them at all to know that they are there. I either sense their presence, or I channel their guidance, which comes in the form of words that I am compelled to pass on or as symbols.

'Sometimes the urge to pass on a message is so strong that I can't stop it. There have been times when I had to pursue a stranger through the supermarket to pass on an important message! It's not always easy working on the side of the angels! Recently, I was telling a friend about the time I felt compelled to pass on a message to a woman that I was standing next to in a shop. Normally, I wouldn't repeat anything that I had been told about another person, and invariably I forget what I have said as soon as it has passed my lips, but this was so unusual that I felt I had to describe the incident to my friend. Then I discovered why I had done so. The lady that I had given the original message to turned out to be my friend's mother!

'Angels do not exist to provide us with parking spaces or make our decisions for us. They are the medium that delivers the message that we need to take responsibility for our own development. We have the power and all the answers within ourselves. Angels awaken us to that reality and then we are on our own.'

Pamela suspects that angels might not be a separate species, as such, but simply a more developed aspect of ourselves and that we are all, in essence, angels in the making.

'When I am healing I often work with a part of the aura that extends from the upper back downwards and could be said to take the shape of wings. We know that the halo depicted in religious pictures is symbolic of the radiance of highly developed individuals and I believe that the idea of an angel's wings originated in the same way. When I am healing I can often sense the strength and shape of these "wings". Furthermore, if an individual has been subjected to persistent physical violence or has suffered mental and emotional distress this can distort and contaminate the aura, which a healer can see as discoloration, distortion or imbalance.'

One of the simplest ways of working with angels in healing is to visualise colours.

'I have been working with colours for fifteen years and it is extremely effective. Anyone can do it. All they have to do is ask the person who needs healing to sit in a chair and then the healer stands behind them. It is not necessary to touch them. You don't even need to put your hands on their shoulders as you can channel the energy into their aura and it will go where it is needed. Then you ask the angels to give you the colour that person needs and it should appear in your Third Eye. You tell your patient to visualise that colour and then breathe it in.

'Healers can get stuck with believing that they have to follow a set pattern of stimulating each chakra in turn and working with their associated colours, but I think a good healer should work intuitively. Sometimes my patients have seen my angel helpers as big baubles of light and later remarked what a beautiful experience they had.

'Whenever you need healing, cleansing or a top-up of energy, just visualise white light entering your body and the angels will follow.'

Although angels can appear anywhere and at any time, Pamela believes that there are certain places where they can be seen more easily.

'Angels like stone circles and ancient sites where nature spirits were acknowledged and worshipped. I have seen remarkable displays of angelic energy at Stonehenge, at Glastonbury Tor and at Avebury, because these are points of great natural energy. Either they mark points on a ley line or they were built over a large deposit of crystals. At Stonehenge I had a message impressed into my mind to stand at a certain place and I saw a vision of radiant colours in the sky. But the site is now so commercial that it is no longer as conducive to sightings. At Glastonbury I stood at the bottom of the Tor with another medium and we picked up the presence of elementals (nature spirits). When we looked up we both saw large pink balls of light coming up out of the Tor.'

One of the least known aspects of angel work is the process known as 'soul rescuing' in which a medium 'clears' a haunted building or site from the presence of earthbound spirits.

'What is sad is when someone cannot return to the light after their death because they are so attached to their life. I have cleared several houses where there have been disturbances or where the owner complains that they cannot live there because a certain room is cold even in the summer. They call me in and the first thing I pick up on is a thickness in the atmosphere as if it is charged with an invisible presence. Sometimes the angels will give me different colours and I will see that spirit taken up through the rays of colour by the angels into the light and then the atmosphere will clear as if the room has been aired. I used to take the spirit up through my own body as I thought that I had to act as a channel for its return to the light but now the angels do it for me. Which is just as well as it could be very exhausting to be a host to someone else's spirit even for a few minutes. I would feel huge and occasionally, if they were reluctant to go, I would still have them with me when I went home. My daughter is very psychic and she would see me hobbling down the garden path, bent double like an old hag with a spirit on my shoulder and calmly say to her dad, "Mum's back and she's brought a ghost home."

'I don't feel any fear when I do soul rescuing, otherwise I couldn't do it. I know the angels are assisting me and it is work that needs to be done. Unfortunately they are too eager to build anywhere these days and most of my work comes from people who have bought new houses built on the site of old burial grounds.

'You have to treat earthbound spirits as if they were still alive as they are the same personalities that they were in life. I once had to persuade the spirit of a pipe-smoking stubborn old man to pass over by promising him that he would have all the tobacco he could smoke if he went over to the other side!'

Pamela has the strongest sense that now is the time when we will witness a greater degree of contact with the angelic worlds.

'I think it is significant that we are seeing a marked increase in the influence of the angels now as the world goes from crisis to crisis. There is a proliferation of songs, films and TV series about angels and the supernatural which suggests that we are becoming more conscious of other realities and that the veil between the worlds is becoming thinner. We need to be conscious of our place and purpose in existence and of the karma we are creating for ourselves in our future lives. One of the lessons that the angels are teaching us is that we cannot judge others as we have doubtless made the same mistakes in previous lives. Angels are here to teach us tolerance and compassion.

'Of course, they can also intervene in a more direct way to save us from physical danger. I have been saved from certain death on more than one occasion. A few years ago I was on a slip road joining the M25 to the M1 when a lorry came up fast on my right side and tried to cut across in front of me. It was about to crush me against the barrier. But before I could react I found myself on the M1 with no lorry in sight. As far as I'm concerned that was a miracle.

'But it wasn't the only time. I frequently had to drive long distances in my job and occasionally I was so tired that I fell asleep at the wheel. I would wake up and find the car was travelling in a straight line as if invisible hands were steering it for me. It isn't as crazy or uncommon as you might think. The American actress Shirley MacLaine tells of a similar incident in one of her books when a voice told her to take her hand off the wheel as she was driving down a winding mountain road. I wouldn't suggest that anyone does that, but it was an important lesson for me. It demonstrated the need for absolute trust in a higher power.

'Once you have seen an angel, you never forget it or the feeling of awe that overwhelms you. The sense of their presence is too much to take in and that is why people become emotional when they recall their experience. I don't feel the need to categorise them or attribute human qualities or specific powers to particular angels. That only weakens the contact. The secret of making contact with the angels is trust, knowing that they are with you and that they will answer you if you ask for and acknowledge their assistance.

'Occasionally I get a message saying that certain people have been sent to me to bring me the help that I need and that they are my angels. So, I suppose that we are all fallen angels in a sense.'

Angels inc.

Kim Arnold, a renowned tarot teacher and organiser of the annual International Tarot Conference in London, readily acknowledges the part angels have played in her success story.

'In 1999 I was struggling with the idea of buying a small shop to sell esoteric items such as tarot cards, crystals and books. But the thought of borrowing heavily from the bank and taking on all the responsibility that goes with refurbishing a small shop was taking a toll on my health. I was becoming a nervous wreck. I'd found suitable premises but they needed so much work and money spending on them that I was seriously thinking about abandoning the whole idea, which had been a life-long dream for me.

'I couldn't sleep for worrying. Then one night as I lay awake I saw a white light appear at the bottom of the bed. It didn't have a face or wings but I knew intuitively that it was what we call an angel. I had never considered asking the angels for help. I suppose I didn't really think they were real at the time, which made it all the more remarkable that I should see it when I really needed reassurance that I was on the right path. It didn't speak but I sensed its power and I felt such confidence from that moment on. It had effected a change in me, a shift in perception. It was definitely a being of energy with a distinct personality and presence of its own and not a projection from my unconscious or a dream. I was wide awake.

'I have seen spirits since I was a child, but this was quite different. Spirits come and go and leave little more than a memory of a sighting, but this being had a presence that resonated within me. It changed me and even friends who knew nothing of my experience would comment on the fact that I looked different – radiant and happy – for days afterwards. That's what an angel encounter does for you if you are lucky enough to have one. And once you have one, you don't need another. You know they are all around you even if you can't see them.'

The day after her angelic encounter Kim found another suitable property for sale and it proved to be ideal. It was in a less prominent location, but it didn't need as much work doing to it and so Kim was able to invest more of her bank loan in acquiring stock, including plenty of angel items!

'Our most popular items are angel cards. There are many on the market and they all seem to help people to make a connection because they have inspiring pictures and words of wisdom which can motivate you if you're feeling low or uncertain which course of action to take. I don't think they are chosen at random. I really believe that there is an invisible guiding hand selecting the card you need for that moment. The only time I don't get an accurate reading using angel cards or the tarot is when people are deliberately blocking me from tuning in – either because they don't really want me to know what is going on in their life, or because they are cynics and want to test me. They sit there with folded arms and challenge me to prove them wrong!'

Kim doesn't feel the need to have her belief in the existence of angels confirmed with another sighting. It is enough that she experiences their influence in her life whenever she needs their help.

'I was recently on a transatlantic flight when we suddenly experienced terrible turbulence. The pilot warned us all to stay in our seats as we rode up and down like a bucking bronco. It was frightening and made me feel physically sick. But then I visualised four angels steadying the plane, one at each wing, one at the nose and one at the tail. A few moments later the turbulence reduced noticeably and the buffeting decreased sufficiently for me to relax.

'Angels are now a central part of my belief system. I see them as an expression of the Divine, but I don't feel the need to perform any specific rituals to attract them. I simply ask them out loud for help and they have always come through for me. I usually ask them for guidance but not for them to resolve something as I believe I should be the one who has to take action.

'I think sometimes people don't get a result when they appeal to the angels simply because they ask for too much. We have to find our own way in life. We can't give responsibility for our future over to higher beings and then just sit back and watch them remove all the obstacles from our path. We wouldn't learn or grow, which is the main reason why we are here on earth. Just imagine what would happen if parents did everything for their children to save them from being hurt or disappointed. What spoilt brats we would be!'

Raising awareness with the angels

Yugoslavian healer Tamara Mount is one of the most remarkable and perceptive psychics that I have had the pleasure of working with. Her personal experiences, together with the insights gained through her work as a qualified counsellor and psychotherapist, have given her a unique understanding of the nature of angels and their place and purpose in existence.

'My understanding is that everything in existence is a manifestation of energy and that the way we perceive that energy – the form that it takes in our mind – depends on our level of awareness. So, a person who is still very grounded in a religion-based culture might perceive higher or stronger energy in the form of angels. People who don't have that conditioning might experience this energy in the form of spirits or ghosts, whereas those who don't share these references and so don't think in such terms might see them as formless emanations of light. Angelic energy appears in a form that the person can understand and with which they will feel comfortable.

'Only by raising our awareness through a conscious effort such as prayer or meditation, or when our faculty for filtering out these higher frequencies is down due to fatigue, only then can we glimpse the greater reality and see that all such phenomena come from within. It is an expression of our true, divine nature. I used to sense spirit guides when I was practising healing, but now I know the power originated in me. It is in all of us.

'This is what Jesus tried to teach 2000 years ago but instead of seeing him as an example of what we could become – a fully realised human being – we worshipped him. However, now people are beginning to accept the possibility that we are each responsible for our own development and cannot attain enlightenment through others, but only through our own increasing self-awareness.

'To manifest the Christ consciousness or guardian angel we have to undergo a form of spiritual detoxification which involves rising through various altered states of consciousness and drawing out the impurities from our psyche. The angels are the messengers who have been sent to wake us up to our innate potential and make a connection with the source. Angels are now appearing in ever increasing numbers to inspire us to accept other realities, to explore and aspire to fulfil our divine destiny.'

Tamara's earliest experiences were similar to those described elsewhere in this book, but as her understanding grew, the experiences became more extraordinary and profound.

'At first, like other people, I had hints which confirmed that we are much more than merely physical beings with a limited life span. I saw ghosts, and odd things happened that played with my perception and understanding of the nature of reality. For example, one day I went to visit my mother-in-law and a friend who was staying with her. As I approached the house I saw through a window the friend coming down the stairs in a red robe to answer the door. But after I rang the bell my mother-in-law answered the door. Her friend was upstairs at that moment, asleep. The next morning I was still in the house when her friend came down the stairs for breakfast wearing the same red robe that I had seen her in the day before.

'Then I began to see angels, but not in the traditional form with wings and a halo. I sensed their presence and felt different degrees of heat and cold, and I would see colours. The first time I saw their features distinctly was when I was visiting a church with a friend. I remember being fixed on a green screen, an empty message board, behind the priest who was giving a sermon. I suddenly became aware of a number of disembodied faces in front of the screen. They would change from a Native American Indian to a Chinese and so on as I watched. Then my palm started to itch and when I looked at it, there were the same faces! I thought I was the only one who could see them so I asked my friend to look and she saw them too. Her face was a study! I wasn't frightened. From that moment on I felt like a child with a new toy. It was fascinating and beautiful at the same time. All I could think was, "So this is possible."

'I believe that angels appear when we are ready to receive a stronger energy, as I was that day. Such phenomena signify and confirm the existence of different forms of energy, but some people are scared to acknowledge something which questions their concept of reality and so they suppress their suspicion that it exists, or deny it if they experience something out of the ordinary. My sceptical husband would always try to find a rational explanation for the strange things that would happen around me, such as our son's battery-controlled toys starting up by themselves five minutes before my son would wake up.

'I compare spiritual development to an endless corridor with many doors. If we are willing to explore, one door will open at a time to show us what is possible, but only if we are ready to ask, "What do I need to learn now?" We can't afford to get hung up on one aspect and put our belief in one specific thing. Our development as human beings depends on our acceptance that self-realisation is an endless process with an abundance of possibilities. You can't ask the angels or a guru to give you a quick fix. There is no such thing as luck. We make our own luck by the choices we make. Every day we are bombarded with possibilities, but we are often afraid to take the less familiar path because we are afraid of what may lie in wait ahead to thwart and frustrate us. It is so sad how we limit and restrict ourselves, because there is nothing ahead but the opportunity for change and personal growth. I came to the understanding that I have because I learnt to rely on my intuition and the inner voice which said, "Trust the process".'

For Tamara, the process involves a willingness to identify and acknowledge the attitudes that could be holding us back from realising our potential and then clearing any negative conditioning which we have acquired from the various influences in our life.

'I don't fear having to face my feelings as many people do. I look on the whole process of self-awareness as I would look at reprogramming a computer. I identify the problem by going inward during relaxation, then I call up the data, so to speak, by being completely honest with myself and finally press "Delete" by letting it go. I don't dwell on the source of my unhappiness or ask for meaning. I acknowledge that the issue exists, but then I set myself free so that it no longer has a hold on me.

'I still believe in angels, but I don't relate everything that happens to me to their influence. I believe there is more and I think that we are the source of more miracles than we are at present prepared to acknowledge.'

Angels of the spheres

One of the world's leading authorities on the Kabbalah is Z'ev ben Shimon Halevi. He is the author of several definitive studies on the subject and he continues to lecture around the world. He rarely gives interviews so it is a privilege to be able to add his voice and insights to this book.

I began by asking him how the Kabbalah defines the nature and purpose of angels.

'In the Kabbalistic tradition the archangels and the lesser angels are distinct discarnate entities confined to the upper worlds of Creation (Beriah) and Formation (Yezirah) respectively. They do not manifest in the world of Action (Asiyyah), our physical world. In another age and in another context we might refer to the angels as nature spirits and the archangels as sky gods for there is an angel overseeing every process in the universe. The angel of the storm, for example, will appear and disappear with the storm. But the Kabbalistic concept of creation envisages the upper and lower worlds as interconnecting and where they overlap you have the spirits of the four elements: Earth, Air, Fire and Water.

'Angels are simple personifications of the divine attributes and creative principles in their relative worlds, marshalled under the archangel Michael. The Rabbis of earlier times regarded them as offspring of the Divine but not divine in themselves. Our perception of them has to be symbolic because their true nature is beyond our limited comprehension.'

For this reason Halevi disagrees with the notion that angels could be a projection of our own higher self.

'Human beings are unique. We have the freedom to choose if we want to sink below the animals or rise above the angels. We can create angelic thought forms through intense meditation, but we are of an entirely different order to the celestial angelics. We are in essence individual cells generated in the body of Adam Kadmon, the fully realised human being or Cosmic Man, who is not to be confused with Adam in the Bible. We have the capacity to experience the higher realms through meditation, but the angels cannot move outside their world of influence and are not permitted to interfere in our world. The Holy One is like a parent who knows that it is better to let its offspring learn by his or her mistakes, through experience, rather than continually correcting them. But without human beings there would be no evolutionary process. The universe would exist for no purpose, like a theatre without actors.'

In *A Kabbalistic Universe* Halevi speaks of the archangelic essence of earthly creatures. What exactly does he mean by that?

'The archangelic essence of a Lion, for example, is the idea of a lion which exists in the world of Beriah, the world of Creation. This is the first stage in the process which brings the animal into being. The spirit of the lion contains the quality of that species and it manifests the essence like a blueprint in the upper astral world before it can take form in our own. That creative process belongs to the archangels and the hosts marshalled around them. If we are to grasp the basic concept we need to work in symbols and psychological forms. That is why, for example, we love T.S. Eliot's *Old Possum's Book of Practical Cats*, because he talks in archetypal forms that we can all relate to.

'The archangels are responsible for the grand design of the universe from the smallest particle to human DNA. They manifest certain principles at that level and live in water, rock and in the heavens. We have given them wings to signify that they are not of this earth but in reality they do not possess wings. Why would they need wings if they are not physical beings?'

According to Halevi, you do not need to perform elaborate rituals to make contact with your guardian angel or higher self. You simply need to be attentive and trust your intuition.

'Some years ago I was in the Valley of the Kings in Egypt. As I walked down a steep slope the incline forced me to pick up speed and I soon found myself running. Ten feet (three metres) from the bottom I was tempted to jump when a voiceless voice said, "Don't do that. Egyptian hospitals!" So I pulled myself up short and was saved from breaking a few bones.'

Why does Halevi discourage his pupils and readers from petitioning the angels and instead urge them to appeal directly to the Divine?

'Because that is magic and magic is forbidden by the Kabbalah. I'll give you an example of what can happen and in fact did happen to a group who practised ritual magic during the Second World War. They made their preparations, attired themselves in their ceremonial robes and performed an elaborate ritual according to an old grimoire (book of magic). They invoked Mars so that they could petition it to intervene on the side of the Allies and were promptly killed when a bomb landed on their temple.

'You have to think of angels as being like cosmic plumbers. They do what they are told to do by the boss. You can appeal to God and He will decide what to do, if anything is to be done. If I can put it in another way, you shouldn't worship the ministers who are aligned to the left and right of the emperor as they have their own agenda and will respond in the way they consider appropriate. Instead, you need to go straight to the emperor and let him decide what to do. And if he decides to intervene he will give it to the appropriate minister.

'I'll give you an example of how appealing to a particular entity can work against you. When I was a young ambitious writer I was increasingly frustrated by the amount of rejection slips that I was getting from various publishers. So, I appealed to Mercury as the messenger to speed things up for me. The next day I went to the post office with my manuscript and found myself at the back of a long queue. But within a few minutes all the people had dealt with their business and I was at the front. I thought, "Great, it works." Within 48 hours I had a reply from the publisher. It was another rejection. That taught me a valuable lesson. You cannot influence events to your advantage by appealing to a minion, you have to go to the master. The minion will do its job, but it will react without considering the implications. In my case, Mercury sped things up but the result was the same. The pattern was not altered until I took my case to a higher court, so to speak.

'Another good example is that of the young man who petitioned Venus to intervene in his love life. The next month he got all the action he wanted. He was pursued by two women, one of whom was an athletic yoga teacher and within weeks he was burnt out, drained of vitality and fit for nothing.

'On a more serious note, if you attune to an entity you can become possessed or psychologically unbalanced. We are like receivers and if we tune into a particular frequency on which the angel or planet of our choice is operating we could be overwhelmed by its signal and our psychological balance could be disturbed.

'You can acknowledge and respect the angels, but you must not worship them.'

He is against invoking angels even with the best intentions.

'It is not right to interfere in the lives of other people, even if you think you are helping them by doing so. Let me give you the example of a group of healers who wanted to help their friend Charlie to become more decisive. They gathered together in a circle and appealed to the angels to help their friend to make up his mind. A force was generated which was sent out to Charlie and the next day they heard that he had shot himself. He had left a note saying how relieved he was finally to have the strength of mind to end it all.'

Having said that, Halevi does not object to the presence of spirit guides if they come through their own volition.

'In the Kabbalah we call these the Magid. They can be a higher aspect of yourself or in some cases a grandparent who has passed over, or even a friend of the family. Often when I am writing I will sense a presence in the room. They come when it is appropriate. The first time I experienced this, I was sitting in meditation when I sensed a presence. I asked it, "Why are you here?" and a voiceless voice in my head answered, "Because I did this too", meaning that he had been a writer. So I asked, "Do I know you?" and my eye instinctively went to the bookcase to a book my father had bought me. There was the name of my guide clearly printed on the cover. But I wanted proof. So I asked where he was born and I immediately had a mental picture of an exotic location, which I recognised from the architecture and the type of landscape, although I hadn't been there. The next day I went to the library and looked at an old guidebook of the region and there was the same picture I had seen in my mind. I later visited the town and found a statue erected in his memory. That is the kind of confirmation you need before you make statements about guides and guardian angels.'

5

Contacting Your Guardian Angel

M any people find it difficult to believe in angels either because they have had no personal experience of angelic intervention, or because they believe that angels are simply 'too good to be true'. Even those who would like to believe in the existence of angels can have difficulty making contact for reasons of which they may be unaware. So the first step in establishing contact is to identify what, if anything, might be interfering with your efforts to make a connection.

Exercise: Clearing

Sit quietly with a notepad and a pen on your lap, close your eyes and focus on the rhythm of your breath.

When you feel suitably relaxed and your mind is quiet, say the word 'Universe' to yourself three times with a pause between each word. Accept whatever images or thoughts come spontaneously into your mind. Do not try to analyse them. Then open your eyes, write 'Universe' on your notepad and beneath this a description of the images or a list of the thoughts that you had.

Now, close your eyes, relax and say the word 'Life' three times with a pause between each word. When you have done this, open your eyes and again make notes.

Repeat this process with the following words while allowing yourself to go deeper into your unconscious each time: 'Love', 'Hope', 'Fear', 'Angels', 'Contact' and finally, your first name.

You will not need a degree in psychology to analyse the insights obtained through this simple word-association exercise, but you may be surprised by what it reveals. Even people who express a belief in angels can harbour unconscious doubts and anxieties which limit their ability to contact higher benign beings.

The following responses are typical: 'Why would an angel want to make contact with me?', 'Angels are too highly evolved to concern themselves with human affairs' and 'Angels only appear to people who are spiritually advanced.' All three statements reveal a lack of self-worth and also a popular misconception. Angels appear to people of all races, ages, religions and beliefs – even those who don't believe that angels exist!

Another common response is, 'What if it forces me to face my fears and repressed memories?' First of all, angels are an expression of unconditional love and come in response to a need for your highest good. They never force anyone to experience anything against their will. If you have a fear of facing your true feelings then it suggests that something needs clearing, and meditating on angels in private or in the company of supportive friends is the safest and most effective way of resolving these issues.

And then there is, 'I only believe in what I can see and experience for myself.' This response suggests a fear of losing control over your own life as a result of having your world view questioned. To the rational mind, anything that cannot be subjected to scientific analysis cannot possibly exist. And yet, scientists are continually discovering elements of our world that appear to defy the accepted physical laws, such as dark matter (which is so small it can penetrate solid objects) and the paradox of quantum physics. Fortunately the laws of the universe do not require our approval before they can operate.

And then there are the responses that indicate a fear of the unknown. Examples being, 'There are malevolent entities out there', 'I'm afraid of what I might attract if I explore such things' and 'It is not right to dabble with things we don't understand or are not meant to contact.' All of these are understandable, given the kind of conditioning many of us have been subjected to through superstition, religious indoctrination and the supernatural nightmares generated in popular culture. However, there is no reason to assume that there is anything malevolent 'out there'.

Angels and intuition

Although formal exercises are an effective technique for attuning to the angels, there are other methods which do not require you to sit in silence or conduct a ritual of any kind. The simplest of these is to trust that still, small voice within, which the mystics call the higher self or guardian angel, but which most people would think of as simple, old-fashioned intuition.

But if you are to act on intuition you need to be aware that there is another voice which can undermine your efforts for self-awareness and personal growth. It is the voice of self-gratification, which Freudian psychologists would call the ego and the self-help gurus would label 'the inner child'. Needless to say, this self-centred aspect of our personality has no truly negative aspect. It is not our shadow nor a separate part struggling for our soul, but nevertheless it is a lower aspect of ourselves, which is immature, lazy and capable of diverting us from the spiritual path if we indulge it. It is the same part of our personality that dismisses all spiritual and psychic experience as a product of the imagination, for it is that facet of our psyche through which we perceive the physical world. And it cannot conceive of another, greater reality which challenges its view of the universe. It is this constant struggle between the lower and higher self which is symbolised in the Old Testament fable of Jacob's struggle with the angel (Genesis 32:24).

In time you will be able to distinguish between these two voices or impulses, but initially you may need to question the source of these impulses and ideas by asking yourself if it is prompting you to pursue something you want or something you need.

Perhaps you will have an impulse to contact a friend or family member and if you do so you will find that they had just been thinking about you and wanted you to call. That is an example of your angel and theirs connecting. The more you act on this impulse, the more often it will occur and the stronger your intuition will become.

We tend to think of women as being more intuitive, but that is simply because they are more inclined to act upon their intuition. Men are equally as intuitive but are conditioned to dismiss intuition as being of no practical use.

Perhaps you have a notion to approach a company regarding the possibility of securing a more satisfying job, but the thought of rejection scares you. Maybe you want to pursue a creative idea, but a nagging voice of doubt has been preventing you. Don't listen to the lower self, which has no aspiration and seeks security in the familiar. It is afraid of change and yet only through change and challenge can we become self-aware and fulfil our potential.

If you could connect with your angel when you are having these negative thoughts it would tell you that there is no such thing as not being good enough. You are, in essence, divine, and you have chosen to incarnate in order to experience the fullness of what life has to offer you.

Exercise: Angelic awareness

Angels do not exist on the same vibrational frequency as we do and so we need to raise our awareness through exercises such as this one. We need to be 'grounded' in order to function effectively in the physical world, but unless we develop an awareness of the higher states of consciousness we risk becoming preoccupied with material things to the exclusion of more subtle influences, and will remain unconscious of our true nature.

The following exercise will help to make you aware of angelic intervention in your life and should be practised on a regular basis – ideally once a month.

Take a piece of paper and a pen or pencil, make yourself comfortable, then close your eyes. Sit quietly for a few moments with the pen and paper in your lap and recall a time in your life when you were saved from physical danger. Perhaps there was more than one occasion. When you have the image in your mind, open your eyes and write a brief description of the incident.

Now close your eyes and try to recall an occasion when you were saved from making a disastrous decision by what appeared at the time to be an intuitive feeling of unease or disquiet. Perhaps there was a time when you almost bought the wrong house, made a long-term commitment to the wrong person or accepted the wrong job? Again, when you have the details clear in your mind open your eyes and make a brief note.

Finally, close your eyes, relax and recall a time when you appeared to have been guided to make the right choice when buying a home, meeting a new partner or friend or finding the right job.

When you have completed your list, sit quietly for a few minutes looking at your notes and consider if these significant incidents were a mere coincidence, as you had once thought, or if they might have been examples of angelic intervention. If you consider them to be merely fortunate then ask yourself what is your definition of 'luck'.

Exercise: The nightly review

The following exercise is a natural extension of the previous one. Again it serves to raise your awareness of angelic influence in your life, but it also clears any negativity and processes the confusion of impressions from the day so that you can have a more peaceful sleep.

It is ideally performed in bed just before you are ready to go to sleep.

Close your eyes and with each breath repeat the phrase 'Calm and relaxed.' Then when you feel in a deep state of relaxation, visualise the events of the day from this point back to the moment you woke up in the morning. Do not re-live the events, as you risk intensifying the emotions connected with them. Instead observe the day and your part in it with detachment. Put yourself in the position of your guardian angel or higher self and observe your actions, reactions, thoughts and conversations from the perspective of a spiritual counsellor or best friend. Can you see moments when you were guided by the still small voice of your guardian angel? Did you experience moments of inspiration and insight that could not have been the result of purely intellectual reasoning? If you had difficulties during the day, how would you have acted differently had you known what effect your actions would have on yourself and others? What advice would you give yourself in order to avoid confrontation or similar misunderstandings in the future?

Remember your guardian angel does not judge you. It offers its observations for your greater understanding and to help you to avoid unpleasant experiences in the future. It does not acknowledge the term 'mistakes', as all experiences are for the enrichment of the individual and the greater understanding of the group soul to which we belong.

Attracting angels

Angels are all around us, but they draw closer whenever we engage in something which strengthens our connection with their world or which awakens our higher self. For example, they watch over us when we are cultivating our gardens, playing with our children and pets, enhancing our homes, learning, teaching and healing. They accompany us when we care for the elderly or sick, engage in any form of creativity, or perform a physical discipline, such as sport, swimming or dance. And when we expand our awareness by meditating, exercising our imagination and contemplating beauty in all its forms (in nature, music and so on) they are close by.

Angels are attracted by our spontaneity, our potential for playfulness and the enjoyment we derive from sharing our life with our friends and family. They love the sound of laughter, which they hear as a form of music, and prayer, which is said to send music-like vibrations into their world. But a picnic or party which ends up with the host in a foul mood because the family didn't contribute according to his or her rules and at which the guests feel forced to appreciate the effort that has gone in to it, is unlikely to attract any celestial company!

Asking the angels

We are all familiar with the expression, 'If you don't ask, you won't receive' and you might also have heard of the biblical entreaty 'Knock and it shall be opened unto you.' Well, there is truth in both, at least when it applies to appealing to the angels.

Angels do not intervene in human affairs unless we appeal to them for help because they must respect our free will and the universal law of cause and effect (karma) under which we live. Contrary to popular belief, angels do not exist to rescue us from danger or solve our everyday problems. Their purpose appears to be to assist in the process of spiritual and physical evolution and they only intervene when our personal development or that of the greater good is jeopardised. Even when we take the initiative and ask for their help they do not always appreciate the urgency of our situation as they exist in a non-physical realm where there is no sense of time. Besides, what is important to us at this moment might be irrelevant to our overall pattern of progress through life and after life.

So, if you want the angels to illuminate your true path in life or intercede for you in a misunderstanding, or perhaps even help you to find a more fulfilling job, then you have to make your message clear and concise. You cannot afford ambiguity and you will have to choose your words carefully to acknowledge the possibility that what you want is not necessarily what you need. For example, if you ask for a more satisfying and fulfilling job with shorter hours, greater potential for promotion, higher wages and less stress you are more likely to succeed than if you ask for 'a better job'. But whilst it is important to define precisely what you want, wherever possible you should leave the details to those who have your best interests at heart. Whilst it is good to know what you want, you can exclude promising possibilities if you are too inflexible. So if you want a more satisfying job, for example, appeal to the angels as you would an employment agency. Don't be shy to tell them your strengths and detail your experience, then ask them to provide something worthy of your abilities in which you can develop in every way. Feel free to add conditions but you should always express a willingness to go where it is right for you to go. The same applies if you seek a new partner or a new home. Apply to the celestial introductory agency or the celestial estate agency but don't neglect to take the necessary practical steps. Act in the belief that you will receive help and that new job, partner and home could be yours before the year is out!

Forms in which guidance may be given

We live in the densest dimension of matter whereas angels exist on a finer frequency and so their influence on our lives is often subtle. It is therefore unrealistic to expect a direct response to every question that you ask them, although you will develop an ability to hear this inner voice as your awareness increases with practice. In the meantime, you may find the following exercises provide sufficient proof of your strengthening connection with the angels.

○ Ask for guidance in the most specific and unambiguous way you can. Then choose a book by instinct and turn to a page at random. Expect to find the answer there and you will.

○ Ask for guidance and then watch out for happy coincidences which appear to offer the answer you needed.

○ Ask that you receive an answer to your question within the next ten minutes and then turn on the radio. Leave it at the station that it has been tuned to and you should hear the answer in a song or something the presenter says, or perhaps even in an advert.

Don't ask how such things are possible or whether there is a rational psychological explanation. I am perfectly content to accept the possibility that our unconscious is highly selective when it comes to highlighting what it wants us to hear or read. But it works more frequently than mere chance would allow. Perhaps an angel is sometimes simply a convenient generic term for those inexplicable incidents in which we help ourselves to find the answers.

Exercise: Channelling

If you want more concrete evidence of the existence of angels, why not ask for it in writing? Yes, it is possible to ask your angels to dictate their messages to you. In the heady days of Spiritualism following the First World War, this phenomenon was known as automatic writing; more recently it is often referred to as channelling. Unfortunately the practice has acquired a rather dubious reputation due to those attention-seeking individuals who claim their communications were channelled from an extraterrestrial! It is my understanding that the source is either a discarnate spirit or the channeller's own guardian angel or higher self and that there is, in my experience, no danger of being influenced by disturbed discarnate spirits if you follow the routines described for grounding (see pages 63–4) and clearing (see pages 47–8).

If in doubt as to the true origin of the message just remember that angels and spirit guides never use modal verbs! They are non-judgemental so words such as 'should', 'must' and 'ought to' are not in their vocabulary. A genuine communication from the angels will offer unconditional love, understanding, reassurance, guidance and insight. Angels respect your free will and will never tell you what to do.

Sit in a comfortable upright chair with a notepad and a pen in your lap. Close your eyes and relax into a steady rhythm of breathing. See the paper in your mind and visualise yourself writing the following sentences while saying them to yourself:

'I am an open, clear and receptive channel for communications from my guardian angel. What is your message of love for this day?'

Wait in silence and stillness for a minute then open your eyes and write down whatever comes into your mind. If no thoughts or impressions appear, write 'nothing'. If you receive what you think is nonsense write it down regardless, as this is part of the unblocking process. Do not analyse what you receive or you risk stopping the flow.

If you receive an uninterrupted flow of thoughts then keep writing until it comes to a natural conclusion. Otherwise, close your eyes and repeat the process. You can do this up to 22 times in one session.

Do not be surprised if it takes several sessions to establish a connection, but be confident that it will come as your angel is constantly trying to communicate with you and will not fail to take the opportunity if you show yourself willing to meet it half-way.

When you receive a communication you will be able to tell immediately if it is genuine as you will find yourself writing faster than you can think about the torrent of thoughts which come into your mind.

An angel journal

It is important to keep a record of your experiences as you complete each of the exercises because you will find that the impressions gained in visualisation invariably fade from the memory like dreams. Moreover, the significance of the symbolism might not be apparent until later on. You may even discover that each symbol provides a piece of a much bigger picture and you will not be able to make the connection unless you have kept a record to which you can refer.

An angel journal, however, can be much more than merely a record of your angelic experiences and your progress as you become increasingly aware of their influence in your life. It can also be a scrapbook, with pictures to inspire and remind you of friends, family and places you love. This is not a sentimental indulgence, it is a magical process. Whenever we generate loving thoughts, our Heart chakra (or centre) is stimulated, etheric energy is circulated throughout the body and the aura expands, attracting the angels to our side. In this way we set up a cycle which produces more opportunities to increase our prosperity. In psychological terms it means that by counting our blessings we create more good fortune for ourselves.

Here are some more suggestions for what to include in your journal and how you can use them to strengthen your contact with the angels.

Angel stories

For an instant fix of angel energy there is nothing quite as direct and effective as reading a true account of an angel encounter. They are far more potent than any anti-depressant currently on the market and there are no side effects. Reading about angelic intervention can also have a physical effect as contemplation of any kind can stimulate the release of endorphins (nature's natural painkillers), which has a calming effect on the brain. So, whenever you hear or read about a particularly moving experience note it down, or cut it out and paste it in your journal. Now that we have the internet there is no shortage of stories to be found. Check out www.guideposts.com or any of the other resources listed in the back of this book.

Heavenly reminders

In the late 1970s a British group had a big hit with a song called 'Reasons To Be Cheerful'. It was basically a witty monologue listing the singer's favourite things and it was guaranteed to raise a smile from even the most humourless person. What many casual listeners didn't know was that the singer, Ian Dury, was disabled and he has since died. Despite his disability, Dury resisted the temptation to indulge in self-pity. Instead he dedicated his creative life to chronicling the quirks of the human condition and cheered us up in the process. By following his example and listing everything that gives you pleasure, you too will have the means to raise your spirits and laugh at the absurdities of life. The angels do not want us to be over serious and treat them with earnest reverence.

There is a Scottish saying which sums this approach up nicely: 'The angels can fly because they take themselves lightly.' And so should we. So feel free to paste in pictures of your favourite comedians, jokes, holiday postcards, family photos, a loving letter from a partner or friend. Anything that gives you pleasure and reminds you how good life can be is eligible for inclusion.

'Giving' lists

We appeal to the angels whenever we want something and that is fine, so long as we are asking for something that we really need for ourselves or for others. But it can strengthen our case if we give something back. The angels do not need anything from us, but they are surely aware of how we demonstrate our love and compassion for others. So, make a list detailing how you give pleasure, practical help or guidance to others and make a point of adding to that list on a regular basis. In short, if you want to attract the angels, then act like one.

Write a reminder in your journal to donate something useful and of value to charity perhaps once a week or once a month, but don't be tempted to use charities as a convenient dump for your old bric-à-brac. Don't short-change the angels.

Life list

Write down the following seven category headings and underneath each one list all the things that you have achieved no matter how trivial they may appear. List as many achievements as you like. It is remarkable how easily we forget our past successes in the mistaken belief that we are only as good as our present job, or current prospects. By recalling seemingly trivial incidents from childhood, such as the time when you overcame your fears or learnt to swim or ride a bike, you will strengthen your self-belief and acknowledge the assistance of the angels, who will be more likely to assist you again when you need them. Don't get hung up on academic achievements. Think instead in terms of the times you have helped other people or overcome some difficulty or exceeded your own expectations.

The categories are:

○ personal qualities

○ career

○ money

○ lifestyle

○ relationships

○ self-expression

○ personal growth.

Now commit as many of these to memory as you can so that when you petition the angels for guidance or practical help you can preface your appeal with gratitude for what you have already achieved. This will increase your expectation of future success and also acknowledge the help you received in the past, demonstrating to the angels that you do not take their assistance for granted.

Note: Remember, this is your private journal and no one should be allowed to see what you have written. It is a tool for self-empowerment and its efficacy will be diminished if you allow it to be coloured with someone else's opinion.

Creating an angel sanctuary

Angels can appear wherever and whenever they choose, but if you wish to be able to summon them to your side whenever you require reassurance, guidance or protection then you will need to create a conducive atmosphere in which to welcome them. This can be done either on the inner planes of the spirit by raising your level of consciousness though visualisation (see Chapter 7), or in the physical world by creating a sacred space in your home. Ideally, you should work on both levels simultaneously, creating with each successive meditation a special place in your home, which will become charged with your personal energy and that of your guardian angel. It will also serve as a place to revitalise you whenever you are feeling low in body or spirit as, over time, it will acquire a rarefied atmosphere as do many places of worship, meditation and healing.

You can create a sacred space in a corner of your bedroom or study with candles, crystals, incense, fresh flowers and appropriate ornaments such as angelic statuettes. In time this area will become charged with your positive mental energy and a sense of peace, making it ideal for quiet contemplation.

But remember:

○ Clutter is not conducive to concentration. A single central object should be your focus. If your room looks like a New Age jumble sale it will prove a distraction and defeat the object of the exercise.

○ If you use candles take particular care as you will have your eyes closed for up to twenty minutes during meditation and you do not want to be distracted by intrusive thoughts concerning fire safety. So ensure that they are secure and that the holder is set in a saucer of water in case of an accident.

○ If you are using candles or incense, the room should be well ventilated as these consume oxygen and can lead to drowsiness and headaches.

○ Not everyone responds to sitting in silent reflection for long periods of time so consider the use of a cassette or CD player as appropriate music, recorded visualisations and natural sounds can be very helpful in creating a conducive atmosphere.

6

Making Contact in Meditation

Not everyone can expect to encounter an angel in their lifetime, and certainly not if they simply sit back and wait for one to appear. The majority of angelic encounters are triggered by a crisis, a moment of imminent danger or despair. It is then that the presence of the angel brings comfort, unconditional love and reassurance that the individual is not alone. It also charges the atmosphere with the air of another world from which it has come. And it is this overwhelming sense of something sacred which remains with the individual for days, causing them to re-evaluate their understanding and perception of reality. Fortunately, you do not need to wait for such a crisis to trigger an angelic experience. Using meditation and visualisations (a form of guided meditation) you can raise your awareness to the angelic realms and attune to their subtle vibrations whenever you wish, whether you need guidance or seek the serenity and security to be enjoyed in their presence.

Even the most naturally gifted mediums and healers acknowledge the importance of meditation for quietening the mind before they open themselves to a higher influence, otherwise they risk being confused by impressions and memories from their own subconscious mind or overwhelmed by impressions in the ether. This ability to 'see' beyond the physical dimension, which we call clairvoyance, is not a superhuman power, but an innate sensitivity to the subtle energies around us, including the presence and influence of the angels. But as with every talent, it needs nurturing. Meditation is the key to exploring and developing clairvoyance and other forms of psychic sensitivity safely. Without it you will be what the great Hindu master Krishnamurti called 'a blind man in a world of colour', surrounded by angels but oblivious to their presence.

Those new to meditation should be reassured that there is no need to feel anxious for any reason. During the following exercises you are always in control. You are not dabbling in the occult, or communicating with spirits.

Meditation merely offers the means by which you can quieten the restless conscious mind so that you will be able to hear the still, small voice within.

The standard definition of meditation as 'an act of reflection and contemplation' is inadequate to convey the serenity that can be experienced when the body is relaxed, the restless mind is at peace and one enjoys a blissful state of well-being, which results from being attuned to the higher self or guardian angel.

Contrary to popular belief, meditation is not the exclusive preserve of religious ascetics or those who are 'spiritually advanced'. However, it can be difficult for beginners who often find that sitting in silence and emptying the mind is not as simple and easy as they had imagined. But it will come quickly and effortlessly if you let go of all thoughts and simply immerse yourself in silence. Don't think about how long you will meditate for and don't anticipate having any visions or extraordinary experiences. Just enjoy the stillness.

Posture

Meditation can be performed either seated or lying down. If you prefer to lie down on a mat or bed, use a cushion to support your neck. Your arms should be by your side and your legs straight with the feet slightly apart. You might prefer to place your hands over your solar plexus to concentrate energy at this crucial energy centre. If so, form a bowl shape with your fingers entwined and your thumbs touching.

If you prefer to be seated, place your feet flat on the floor and slightly apart in parallel with your shoulders. Your hands can be cupped in your lap as described above or placed palms down on your knees.

Keep your head erect as if you are looking straight ahead, but don't let your chin drop on to your chest because it will restrict the flow of air.

It is not necessary to adopt the traditional postures of yoga and Buddhism although these positions are intended to align the spine in preparation for channelling etheric energy from the chakras and to create a sense of being centred.

To assume the full lotus position, place the right foot on the left thigh and the left foot on the right thigh. With the half lotus the right foot should rest on the left thigh while the left foot is tucked under the right thigh, or vice versa. The quarter lotus requires one foot to lie under the opposite thigh while the other foot is held under the opposite leg.

Alternatively, try a traditional Japanese posture by resting on your heels with a cushion supporting your bottom.

Establishing the habit

It can be difficult initially for Westerners to establish the pleasantly addictive habit of meditation as we are conditioned to believe that we must be constantly active and productive. Setting aside time for ourselves for meditation is still considered by many to be self-indulgent and even somewhat eccentric.

The first step in overcoming this inner resistance is therefore to establish a regular routine by deciding to set aside between ten and twenty minutes every day. If you wait for a convenient time, there will always seem to be something that needs doing more urgently than the meditation.

Note: If you feel uncomfortable at any time during an exercise all you have to do is count down slowly from ten to one and open your eyes. Usually the anxiety has gone before you get to one and so you can resume the meditation. It is perfectly normal to feel apprehensive at times when you begin a programme of self-examination such as this, as the ego resents having its pleasurable distractions taken away and being forced to sit in silence.

Beware of becoming a bliss junkie!

In time you will find that meditation can become pleasantly addictive. But beware! Once you have attained that elusive sense of detachment from the world it is tempting to indulge and lose yourself in the peace and presence of the angels, but if you do so you risk becoming what is known as a 'bliss junkie'. You could have your head permanently in the clouds when it should be dealing with practical everyday matters. Meditation does not offer an escape from our responsibilities. It is a technique for helping us to cope with life and maintain a sense of proportion, a state Buddhists call 'being in the world, but not of it'. So limit your sessions to between 20 and 30 minutes. Remember, the angels will always be there, day and night, and your contact will grow stronger with practice, but if you use your 'time out' with the angels to escape from your responsibilities they will withdraw.

Practical tips for angel meditations

Whatever room you dedicate to meditation you will need to ensure your peace and privacy. If there are other people in the house or flat let them know in advance that this is to be a time when you are not to be disturbed and put a note to that effect on the door. Finally, before each session take the phone off the hook or switch on the answering machine.

It is a good habit to take a shower before meditating as this is said to cleanse the aura of emotional residue as well as attuning the body. Bathing also makes us mindful of the body and impresses the importance of meditation on the unconscious. It is for these reasons that cleansing became a significant element of both esoteric and religious ritual.

It is a good idea to keep a glass of water beside you as it will help to ground you after you return to waking consciousness. You may also find it of practical use as the throat can become dry during prolonged meditation and a cough can become irritating and distracting if you don't have something to relieve it.

Try to avoid eating an hour before meditating as it can be difficult to attain a sense of detachment if your body is busy digesting a heavy meal.

You may find it helpful to record the scripts and descriptions of the longer and more detailed visualisations as they can be difficult to memorise, although eventually it will be sufficient to recall the general outline of the exercise. The details of the inner journey will have been impressed on your unconscious with repeated practice.

Before you can attempt any form of conscious connection with your guardian angel you need to quieten your mind, relax your body and ground yourself. Initially you may wish to approach this process as two separate exercises of between five and ten minutes each until they feel natural and you are comfortable sitting still and in silence with your eyes closed without thinking about which chores need doing. After a few days of practice you should be able to combine breath control and grounding into a single fluid exercise lasting between ten and fifteen minutes after which you can seamlessly move into whichever angel visualisation you choose.

Finally, don't forget to record your experiences in your angel journal after each session as impressions tend to fade as quickly as a dream. Describe the images that have arisen in as much detail as you can as these may have a symbolic significance that you can analyse at a later date.

'Let go even of the idea that you are meditating. Let your body remain as it is and your breath as you find it.' (Sogyal Rinpoche)

Exercise: Breath control

Focusing on the breath is one of the most effective methods of settling the mind in preparation for connecting with your guardian angel. Breath control is also essential for channelling and circulating prana (the breath of life) around the body. Prana is the Hindu term for etheric energy or the life force.

Make yourself comfortable, close your eyes and sense the movement of your breath in your chest and nostrils.

Begin to establish a regular rhythm, inhaling and exhaling for a count of four with a pause for a count of two between each breath. With practice you will find a sense of detachment and serenity in this space between the breaths.

Sustain a blank canvas in your mind for as long and as effortlessly as possible. Do not try to suppress your thoughts. If intrusive thoughts arise, attach no significance to them. We can't control our thoughts, only our response to them.

When you are ready, open your eyes and sit still for a few moments.

If counting is too abstract or boring you can repeat a simple affirmation such as 'calm and centred' or a single appropriate word such as 'angel', for example.

Focusing on the breath is a form of silent meditation and much more difficult and demanding than one might imagine. So be patient with yourself and do not be discouraged if you become distracted in the beginning. Simply bring your mind gently back to the focus of your meditation and continue.

Still waters

It is said that during meditation the mind should be as smooth as the surface of a lake. Use this image to quieten the mind during meditation and when thoughts arise, observe them with detachment as if they are birds crossing the skyline. Then gently draw your attention back to the surface of the lake.

When you can stabilise this image for five minutes you can vary it by visualising a single leaf floating gently down to the surface where it sends tiny ripples spreading out towards the shore.

Resist the temptation to elaborate further, as in meditation the rule is, the simpler the better.

Exercise: Grounding

This exercise is essential if you are to avoid the risk of becoming light-headed and unbalanced by the infusion of energy you will experience during the more advanced visualisations. It must be performed while seated and with your feet planted firmly on the floor.

Make yourself comfortable, close your eyes and focus on your breath.

When you feel suitably relaxed, imagine that you are resting against a mighty oak tree that has weathered the elements for centuries. As you lean back against the thick trunk sense its strength as the sap rises from the roots to the tips of every leaf. The trunk supports you while its branches tower above, shielding you from the heat of the summer sun.

Not even the fiercest storm can topple it for its roots burrow deep under ground and fasten themselves to the earth with a tenacious grip. Now you too can draw your strength from the earth and lose all sense of self as you merge with the oak.

See the soles of your feet blur and blend with the ground as you send fibrous roots of etheric energy deep down into the soil, securing you to the earth. Sense the life force soaking up through these roots from deep within the soil into your lower legs, on into your upper legs and into your back like the life-giving sap that nourishes the tree.

Now imagine raising your arms to the clouds and see them blurring with the branches, soaking up the sunlight which sustains all plant life. Sense the two streams of terrestrial and celestial energy merging within you, regenerating every cell and revitalising the very core of your being.

When you are ready, return to waking consciousness by counting down from ten to one. As you have been deeper in this exercise than before, it is advisable to sit still for a few minutes before resuming your activities.

Closing down

Although it is understandable that you will want to prolong your connection with the angels after your sessions have ended, it is essential that you close down after every exercise. If you do not desensitise yourself you risk being overwhelmed by influences from the other worlds when you need to be focusing on practical matters. I have known 'sensitives' who became so addicted to the natural high of the angelic experience that they chose to remain open at all times. They soon began to hear intrusive voices, after which they were forced to break their connection with the angels and their spiritual development was set back by several years.

To close down, all you have to do is either take a shower, splash cold water on your face and hands, or visualise closing down the chakras beginning with the Crown, then the Brow chakra, followed by the Throat, Heart, Solar Plexus, Sacral and finally the Root or Base chakra below the perineum. Finish by stamping your feet to ground yourself.

Once you have done this you will still experience the sense of well-being and peace of mind which is a result of your angelic connection and, most important, you will bring that heightened awareness into your everyday life. But you will not be acutely sensitive to atmosphere when it could be inconvenient, nor open to the influence of discarnate beings, both of which can complicate life in the 'real world'!

7

Visualisation

T he traditional method for communicating with the angels is, of course, prayer, but effective though it can be, prayer puts the appellant at the mercy of the celestial forces who, we assume, can choose to respond or not, at their whim. That said, subjugating your ego to a higher power can be the most direct and effective method, but many of us find it difficult to surrender unconditionally to something we cannot see and maybe have difficulty believing even exists. To offer a prayer and expect a response takes a leap of faith that is simply beyond most individuals who may not subscribe to a specific religious belief and may feel that they alone are responsible for their fate.

A more self-empowering form of communion with the Divine is to make an invocation, which is similar to praying but involves calling upon a specific angel by name. However, some people may be uncomfortable with this approach because of its associations with paganism and ceremonial magic, or they might simply feel self-conscious at the thought of performing an archaic ritual in which they are required to chant aloud.

Fortunately, there is an alternative technique, which is not only practical and user-friendly for the modern spiritual explorer, but also promises an intimate personal connection with the angels. It is called visualisation and is a form of guided meditation in which you use your imagination to explore the inner landscape of the unconscious or to expand consciousness beyond the physical realms into the spiritual dimension at will.

While both prayer and invocation involve appealing to unseen external forces on a verbal and emotional level, visualisation uses symbols and archetypal images to picture whom you want to contact and therefore offers a more direct and measurable means of connecting with the angelic inhabitants of the mental and spiritual realms.

We have been conditioned to equate imagination (our capacity to create mental images) with idle day-dreaming. However, its primary purpose is to help us to create our own reality by picturing what we desire and then bringing it into being. In this way we can attract a new partner, secure a more fulfilling job, find our ideal home or even heal minor physical ailments, particularly those with a psychosomatic origin.

Its secondary purpose is to facilitate exploration of the inner and upper worlds and to receive impressions of the inhabitants in a form we can accept and understand.

Imagination or reality?

It is relatively simple to distinguish between a product of the imagination and a genuine contact. All you have to do is ask yourself the following questions:

- O Did the image of the angel or archetype appear spontaneously?

- O Did the image appear fully formed with a personality and characteristics of its own?

- O Could I manipulate the image as I would be able to do if it was a creation of my imagination or did it have a life of its own?

- O Did I have a sense of another non-physical presence?

- O Did I have the impression that something was trying to communicate by impressing its thoughts in my mind?

- O Was the quality of the experience distinct from the times when I have simply imagined things?

- O Was I left with an almost physical sense of the sacred, of having glimpsed another world, another reality?

If you answered 'yes' to any of these questions, then you could consider the experience real. In time, with experience, you will not have to ask yourself these questions. You will 'know' intuitively without any measure of doubt that the contact was genuine. What you do with that knowledge and the insights or guidance you gain is, of course, the real point of the exercise.

Basic visualisations

If you find it difficult to visualise, choose one of the following exercises and practise it for five minutes once a day for six days. Then take a break for one day before continuing with the routine for a second week. Even if you find it relatively easy to visualise, these exercises will help you to discipline the mind and develop your innate ability to sustain images, allowing you to access the unconscious at will.

Exercise: The white dot

Make yourself comfortable, close your eyes and relax. Focus on your breath and let all thoughts dissolve, leaving your mind clear and quiet.

You see nothing but black, empty space. Now begin to visualise a small white dot of light in the distance. It is the size of a star. Hold that image for a few moments. Keep the pin prick of light steady against the black background. When you feel you can sustain it for as long as you wish, begin to draw it closer to you until it is the size of a ping-pong ball.

When you can hold this image steady, draw the white sphere nearer until it almost fills the black space and watch as it radiates an intense warming light from within which makes you feel calm and relaxed.

Finally, draw the sphere towards you and absorb yourself in its centre. Enjoy the stillness.

When you are ready to return to waking consciousness become aware of the weight of your body and your surroundings, then open your eyes.

When you feel comfortable with this exercise you can take the next step and visualise yourself passing through the light into the inner world beyond. You can also use this exercise to calm and centre yourself whenever you are anxious or in need of protection.

Exercise: The feather

As your confidence grows you can move on to this second basic exercise which will help discipline your mind and develop your facility for visualisation. Again, it is recommended that you practise this once a day for six days, then take a break for a day before continuing for a second week.

When you are suitably relaxed, visualise yourself in an empty room without furnishings of any kind. If you feel claustrophobic you can visualise a door and windows, but the room should be sparse and plainly painted in a single primary colour so that you are not distracted by details.

When you have this image sustained in your mind, imagine a white feather lying on the floor. With each intake of breath you are going to draw the feather up into the air, hold it suspended in front of you at head height for a moment before allowing it to float gently to the floor as you exhale.

Once you are able to sustain the imagery in these exercises for five minutes you will be ready to move on to the more detailed visualisations in which you can make contact with the angels.

Exercise: Auric wings

Sit in a firm chair with your back straight, close your eyes and take a deep breath. Purse your lips and exhale making a prolonged 'F' sound to expel the last particle of stale air. Now relax into a regular, steady rhythm of breathing.

Become aware of a slight pressure in the middle of your chest which softens your heart centre and radiates outwards to emerge between the shoulder blades. Feel this pressure growing and as it does so, you sense a warm glow beginning to spread across your upper back. Visualise a spiral of sparkling light like a trail of sparks beginning in the centre of this pressure point and radiating outwards as it unfolds. Sense the trail of sparks growing in intensity and the pressure increasing until your upper back is tingling with the emerging etheric energy.

Visualise this energy forming into a pair of wings with the tips almost touching the back of your head and the lower points just above the ground. These 'wings' are symbolic of your divine radiance and an extension of your aura. The angels can see this glow like a beacon in a mist and are drawn to it. That is why whenever you soften your heart centre and expand your aura by radiating love and compassion, the angels draw near to you.

Now visualise this radiance drawing your guardian angel towards you. Sense its presence, which brings peace, reassurance and strength in its stillness. It moves through you, producing a pleasant frisson through your body and stimulating every element of your being.

It now stands behind you. Feel its gentle, reassuring touch as it places its hands on your shoulders. Ask for whatever you need, whether it is guidance, insight, protection or peace of mind. Know that it is your right to ask and to expect its help for it exists to serve the divine will and you are a sublime and complete expression of that will. You are the most evolved form of life on this planet and have nothing to fear.

When you are ready thank your guardian angel, sense the closing of your 'wings' and return to waking consciousness.

The inner sanctuary

If you do not have the space or feel the need to make an angel altar at home you can use visualisation to create an inner sanctuary to which you can return whenever you need to contact your angel. Visualising angels at will takes considerable practice and experience, but if you can visualise a place associated with serenity and stillness it will be much easier to attract the angel to you.

Do not worry if the images are vague at first, or if you cannot sustain the picture of your special place for more than a few minutes. Over time and with practice it will become as real as anything you could construct in the physical world. In fact, it will be more so as the world of spirit is eternal.

Exercise: The walled garden

Make yourself comfortable, close your eyes and enter a state of deep relaxation.

When you are suitably relaxed, visualise yourself sitting in a chair in front of the gently billowing drapes of a set of large french windows. It is a late summer evening and you are lulled into a light trance by the sound of birdsong and the low steady droning of bees in the garden beyond. Through the open window you breathe the heady, intoxicating scent of flowers and freshly cut grass.

A moment later you find yourself rising from the chair and passing through the open door into the soft warm evening sun. You have no sense of the weight of your body. It is as if you are drifting as effortlessly as the air itself.

You enjoy the sensation of weightlessness as you come to rest under the shade of a large fruit tree in blossom. Here under the protection of its hanging branches you can appreciate the stillness of the garden which is alive with flowers of every colour, shape and texture. Now you can see that the colours are more vivid than any in the physical world and, in fact, the quality of light is of another more vibrant world, a world where every living thing appears to be illuminated by a radiance from within. The sun filters through the canopy of overhanging branches and seems to soak into your skin, re-invigorating every cell of your being.

When you have absorbed sufficient energy, you rise and make your way to a short flight of stone steps leading down to a sunken section of the garden out of sight from the main house. As you descend slowly and deliberately, count down from ten to one and say as you go:

'Ten ... I am relaxed ... nine ... down ... eight ... down ... seven ... deeper into relaxation ... six ... calm ... five ... calmer ... four ... light ... three ... lighter ... two ... stillness ... one ... and peace.'

You are now in a formal sunken garden. Take a few moments to familiarise yourself with your surroundings. There is a fountain in the centre. Come towards the fountain and listen to the trickling waters and look into the sparkling sunlight on the surface. As you look deeper into the light a figure appears reflected in the water. When you turn you see it is your guardian angel. Its face is radiant with unconditional love, understanding and compassion. It has come to answer your questions and to offer guidance if you need it.

Ask whatever questions you wish and await the answers which may come as a soft inner voice or you may be given something that is symbolic of what you need. If you don't receive anything, be patient – the answer may appear in your dreams.

When you are ready, count slowly down from ten to one, open your eyes and return to waking consciousness.

You are now ready to use relaxation and visualisation techniques to connect with your guardian angel for healing, guidance and self-awareness.

Healing with the angels

It is generally accepted among both orthodox medical practitioners and complementary health therapists that many common disorders have a psychological source. Often physical symptoms are a manifestation of psychological dis-ease which can be cured simply by identifying the cause of the imbalance and addressing the issue using counselling, hypnotherapy or self-healing as described below. By visualising certain symbols and colours it is possible to programme the unconscious to trigger the required response from the body's own defence system.

In the following pages I list the most common ailments and suggest possible causes and cures using angel visualisations. However, it is important to stress that for all serious, recurrent and persistent ailments you should always consult your doctor.

Exercise: The angel's consulting room

Lie down on your bed or an exercise mat with a small pillow supporting your neck. Close your eyes and relax into a regular rhythm of breathing. As you inhale, say to yourself 'Relax' and as you exhale say 'Release'.

When you are ready, visualise yourself standing before large white double doors, each of which is embossed with a green cross enclosed in a white circle. The circle is also outlined in green so that it stands out against the white of the door.

You enter and find yourself in the reception area of what appears to be a private clinic. Everything is sparkling new and sparsely furnished, suggesting clinical cleanliness and efficiency.

There is a white door to your left and another to your right. Choose one and enter. Whichever one you choose you will find yourself at the top of a flight of steps leading down to a private consulting room.

You walk slowly and deliberately down the steps counting as you descend and saying the following to yourself:

'One ... relax ... two ... release ... three ... down ... four ... deeper ... five ... into relaxation ... six ... down ... seven ... deeper ... eight ... into relaxation ... nine ... going down ... ten ... at peace.'

You pass through the door and enter the consulting room. You may find that it is as clinically clean and sparsely furnished as was the lobby or you may discover that it is a comforting old-fashioned consulting room with shelves of well-thumbed medical reference books and perhaps even a warming fire in the hearth.

You are greeted by a benign figure who welcomes you and puts you at your ease. This is your guardian angel in the form of a medical professional in whose presence you feel comfortable and confident.

You may see your healer in the form of an old-fashioned doctor whom you associate with a reassuring no-nonsense, commonsense kind of approach or as an angelic healing figure of light, radiating compassion. Allow the image to arise spontaneously and assume the form it deems suitable.

In a voice that is soft and reassuring your healer asks you to lie down on a couch and relax. Again you are asked to count down from ten to one while saying the following to yourself, only this time as you do so you gradually lose all sense of your body. You become detached and almost float off the couch.

'One ... relax ... two ... release ... three ... down ... four ... deeper ... five ... into relaxation ... six ... down ... seven ... deeper ... eight ... into relaxation ... nine ... going down ... ten ... at peace.'

Your healer bends down and touches each of the chakra points to stimulate the energy flow and clear any blockages which restrict the flow of etheric energy throughout the body. You now see your body as transparent and radiant from within as the universal life force circulates along the network of meridian lines which carry energy from the chakras to the vital organs. You are feeling re-invigorated and revitalised. Every cell of your being is re-energised. You feel more alive than you have ever done before.

After a few moments you rise from the couch and make ready to leave. Before you go your healer offers a diagnosis and writes you a prescription. You thank him or her and look at the paper you have been given. What does it say?

On the way out the healer pauses at a shelf containing bottles of coloured liquid, natural herbs, ointments and pills. Each is clearly labelled. Which remedy does he or she choose for you? Remember the colour if it is in a solution, as this may be significant.

When you are ready, return the way you came, begin to sense the weight of your body and your surroundings, then open your eyes. Lie still for a few moments considering the significance of what you have seen and sensed before returning to your activities.

Self-diagnosis

In the following visualisations I describe how you can ask for the assistance of the angels in treating the source rather than the symptoms of the most common ailments.

Note: These exercises are designed to treat psychosomatic complaints. If you suspect there is a physical reason for the problem, you are urged to seek medical advice.

Back

The lower back is linked to the solar plexus, which is the emotional centre and therefore persistent aches and pains in this area could be the result of repressing your emotions. The back can also 'lock up' in response to a situation in which we resent having to bear too much responsibility or fear that we might not be able to support ourselves.

VISUALISATION: Imagine your angel standing before you holding a sphere of white light. Watch as it stretches out its arms towards you and sense the warming glow as it presses the sphere into your solar plexus. Feel the warmth massaging your lower back, dissolving the tension and the knots of repressed emotions. Sense the surge of energy which is now coursing through your body. Know that you are never alone and that it is not for you to be weighed down with a burden or with resentment, but to be supported by your guardian angel to whom you can unburden yourself whenever you wish. Understand too that it is your progress that is impaired by harbouring a grievance, resentment or regret. Let it go and move on.

Bladder and bowels

Bladder and bowel ailments such as chronic constipation are frequently associated with control issues which may have originated in early childhood as the only way of guaranteeing parental attention.

VISUALISATION: Visualise a situation in which you and your family or friends are exploring a new town, house or location in the company of your angel who is so large that you are all enfolded in its wings. Sense the security that comes with knowing that you and your home are protected at all times by this awesome being. Know too that the universal life force personified by the angel is eternal and expanding. Every moment a new star is born somewhere in the cosmos. You are not responsible for the course that evolution will take. You are here to enjoy your time on earth and experience the marvel that is existence. If you worry, or try to control people and events, you will miss it.

Ears

Chronic ear infections can be psychosomatic in origin. It could be that there is an unconscious desire to 'turn a deaf ear' to the truth of a situation or to the opinion of other people.

VISUALISATION: Visualise your angel standing by your side next to the affected ear. Watch as it puts its hand to your ear and feel the warmth of its touch as it disintegrates the infected cells and soothes the inflammation. If there is an issue which you cannot resolve or discuss with other people, then confide in your angel and trust that the solution will be forthcoming.

Eyes

Eye infections usually require antibiotics but recurrent problems can be caused by an unconscious wish to 'turn a blind eye' to something we find unpleasant or a need not to have to face reality.

VISUALISATION: Visualise yourself living alone in a dark room. There is nothing to disturb you, but neither is there anything to stimulate your senses. You hear the sound of birdsong and laughing children in the distance. You rise and peek through the curtains. Outside, the sun is shining. It is a late summer evening and the scent of flowers drifts through a crack in the french windows. You draw back the curtains and the sun illuminates the airless room. You are bathed in the universal life force and rejuvinated by its warmth through the glass. You open the french windows and step out into the garden. Your senses are overwhelmed and you feel more alive than you have ever felt before. Explore the garden. Breathe in the intoxicating scent of the flowers and freshly cut grass, see the vivid living colours unlike any on earth, touch the soft velveteen leaves, taste the freshness in the air and affirm that you will never close your eyes to beauty again.

Feet and legs

Problems in the lower limbs are often a physical manifestation of anxieties concerning our ability to 'stand on our own two feet', be independent and support ourselves.

VISUALISATION: Commit this story to memory and, whenever you are feeling low, close your eyes and picture yourself on a deserted beach. Then recall the story in detail.

One night a man was visited by his guardian angel who took him into the celestial realms to show him scenes from his life so far. As the man watched the events of his life being replayed he noticed that there were two sets of footprints on the path for most of the journey where the angel had walked at his side. But at the times of greatest crises and suffering he was surprised to see only one set of prints. So he said to the angel, 'I thought you were my guardian angel, assigned from my birth to love and protect me, but it seems that when I needed you the most you left me to suffer alone.'

To this the angel gently replied, 'Beloved child, I love you and I would never leave you. During those days and nights when you were burdened by sorrow, worry and fear, it was then that I carried you.'

Know that the universal life force is with you literally every step of the way.

Hands and arms

Debilitating disorders such as rheumatoid arthritis can be a manifestation of the mistaken belief that we have no influence on the world around us and so we withdraw into ourselves, making ourselves helpless and vulnerable in an effort to prove that we are indeed as vulnerable as we fear we are.

VISUALISATION: Visualise your hands and arms sealed in a hardening clay. Now see yourself bathing them in a bowl of warm soapy liquid that dissolves the clay, leaving your hands, fingers and arms supple and soft to the touch. The warm soapy liquid permeates the skin, massaging the muscles, lubricating the joints and coating the bones, restoring the feeling to your fingers. Now rinse your hands under a flowing tap of fresh water until every trace of the clay is gone.

Head

Migraines can occur when there is a conflict between the head and the heart (between the intellect and the emotions). They can also manifest in an attempt to elicit sympathy and attention from whoever is the cause of that conflict.

VISUALISATION: Imagine your guardian angel standing behind you holding a radiant sphere of white light above the crown of your head. If this is too difficult to visualise then simply imagine the sphere of light. See it pulsing with the universal life force and know that it is a source of strength for you to draw upon at any time you wish. As the angel lowers it, or as you draw it down into your head, sense the warmth as it eases the tension in your facial muscles and dissolves all anxiety, leaving you feeling relaxed and confident.

Heart and chest

Problems of the heart and chest should always be referred to a qualified medical practitioner, but occasionally minor aches in the chest can be symptomatic of a fear of being constrained or pressure from being under stress.

VISUALISATION: Take a deep breath, hold for a moment, then exhale as slowly and steadily as you can. Expel the very last atom of stale air from your lungs while visualising a cloud of dust being expelled from your chest. Now visualise inhaling the life force in the form of a stream of luminous particles of white or gold. And as you do so, sense the presence of your angel drawing near. Feel its hand on your chest, softening the blockage that you have built up as a defence against stress and anxiety. Give your worries over to the angel and know that all will be well. Let go of the idea that you must control events by force of your will. Relax. Let go. Leave it to the angels. Ask them, in words of your own choosing, to resolve your problems or relieve you of your excess responsibilities. Then see the angel dissolve into the ether, taking your worries with it.

Kidneys

Kidney stones, which disrupt the clearing and filtering process in the body, can be created by an individual who has difficulty processing their emotions, expressing their feelings and facing issues that need to be resolved.

VISUALISATION: Ask your angel to soften your heart centre as described above and ask that it helps you to express in words whatever is troubling you. See the issue raised, discussed and resolved amicably with the person(s) with whom you are having difficulties. Ask for your angel to meet with their angel and resolve the situation for the highest good of both parties (difficult people have guardian angels too!) Finally, see the life force leaving your angel's hand, entering your body and dissolving the kidney stone. Visualise the stone as a small white piece of chalk crumbling in the heat and being washed away, leaving the kidney clear and functioning as it should.

Liver

The liver is concerned with the process of detoxification and maintaining the balance of nutrients in the body. This critical process can be upset by disturbances in the psyche originating from despair, resentment and regret.

VISUALISATION: Select your favourite piece(s) of music and record them on to a cassette or blank CD. Then make yourself comfortable, close your eyes and listen to the music while visualising yourself giving a party for your family and friends in the near future when your present problems have all been resolved. See yourself and your guests happy while the music plays in the background and know that anything you regret is in the past and has no power over the present. Know too that if you resent someone for having something you don't, or for having achieved something you haven't, you are only holding yourself back from acquiring the happiness and contentment to which you are entitled. If you have been depressed, recall a time when you felt like this before and know that it passed and afterwards you took pleasure again in your friends, family and your share of good fortune. If you are lonely, thank the angels for giving you this music, for inspiring whoever wrote it and for leading you to it. Thank the angels for inspiring the people who invented the technology that allows you to hear recorded music whenever you wish. Stop taking everyday miracles for granted and take pleasure in the beauty around you. Even if you don't have much in terms of friends or luxuries, you have a world of possibilities. Lose yourself in the music as you would immerse yourself in a warm, soothing, perfumed bath. That is what music was made for. That is why the angels gave it to us.

Neck and shoulders

Aches in the neck and shoulders are frequently a symptom of a belief that we are shouldering too much responsibility.

VISUALISATION: Visualise yourself carrying your burden. If it's financial, then you might see yourself hauling a sack full of bills. If it is responsibility for the welfare of others, you could see yourself physically carrying your family up a steep hill. Don't get hung up on whether the image is physically possible or not. The stronger the symbolism, the more effectively the message will get through to the unconscious. Then sense the burden becoming lighter as your guardian angel bears you and your burden home. Affirm in words of your own choosing that you are never alone and that whether you are aware of it or not, your guardian angel is there to support you each and every day of your life.

Skin

Eczema is one of the most common psychosomatic disorders and can be an unconscious reaction to something which the sufferer finds irritating to the point where they manifest a desire to get out of their skin. It can also relate to problems associated with self-image or over sensitivity.

VISUALISATION: Visualise yourself enclosed in the wings of your guardian angel. You may sense these as physical feathered wings of white and gold or as an aura of radiant celestial energy. Whichever form it takes in your mind, know that you are enfolded in this protective embrace 24 hours a day, every day of your life. No one walks through life alone and no one has to suffer anything alone or unacknowledged. You may not be aware of this influence in your life, but it is there none the less. When the angel is with you, you are in tune with the divine aspect of your being. The angels have no unrealistic expectations for you to fulfil. You are perfect. You are complete. Right now.

Pain relief

The following visualisation is beneficial for relieving mental and emotional pain as well as physical discomfort. But remember, all serious problems should be referred to a medical professional.

VISUALISATION: Sit in a comfortable chair and allow yourself to sink into deep relaxation. Visualise a white light at the other side of the room and watch as it grows in intensity until it fills the room from floor to ceiling. As you watch it, a figure emerges from the light. It is your guardian angel and it has come in response to your appeal for help. Standing before you, it unfolds its enormous wings and you surrender unconditionally. As you do so, you feel the pain or anguish leave you, slipping off your shoulders like a dirty, worn-out blanket. See the pain as dark matter being drawn out of the core of your being.

The angel has passed through you, relieving you of your burden and replenishing your soul with a vibrant love of life.

Now it stands behind you, wraps you in its wings and transports you to a place of serenity and peace. Here nothing can harm you. The warmth of its wings permeates your body and saturates every cell, penetrating to the very essence of your being, to the source, not just the symptoms.

When you are ready, return to waking consciousness in the usual way.

Exercise: Angel colour therapy

Angels are an embodiment of a particular frequency of energy that exists beyond the range of our physical senses. But we can attune to them using anything that corresponds to that same vibrational frequency if it is transposed to a lower key, to use a musical analogy. Colours, musical notes, crystals and even fragrances are commonly cited as a offering a sympathetic link to a specific angel but, without doubt, colours present the simplest and most direct method of making contact with the angels. I give here specific colours as visual aids for working with each angel, but feel free to use whichever colour works for you.

Begin by focusing on the breath and visualising an earthy brown sphere, which is the colour of the physical plane. Visualising this colour while intoning the name Sandalphon, the angel of the Earth, will help you to be more grounded, pragmatic and less anxious.

Now visualise a bright red sphere while intoning the name of the archangel Gabriel whose name translates as 'strength in God'. This combination will help conquer lethargy, ease bladder and bowel ailments and is even said to dissolve the crystals that cause arthritis. If you lack motivation this is the combination that will stimulate you to get things done and remain committed until you see them through.

Now visualise the colour yellow and repeat the name of the archangel Raphael whose name means 'healing power of God'. Aside from its restorative powers, this combination of colour and the repetition of the name of the corresponding angel can increase your confidence, self-reliance and renew your love of life.

Next, visualise a pulsating orange sphere and repeat the name of the archangel Uriel whose name means 'the light of God'. Allow any knots of suppressed emotions to unravel or blockages to be dissolved. If you become emotional do not try to repress these feelings as they obviously need to be cleared. Raising your awareness to this level can also be effective in eradicating digestive disorders and revitalising the body after surgery or during recovery from a debilitating illness.

Next visualise a pulsating sphere of livid green and intone the name of the archangel Michael whose name means 'like unto God'. As you do so, you should sense the heart centre softening, which will neutralise anger and resentment while cultivating compassion for others. On a purely physical level, it will improve your circulation and reduce the symptoms of stress.

Now visualise the colour indigo and intone the name of the angel Samael whose name means 'contraction of God', which can be interpreted as the quality of reflection. If you need to be less impulsive or are dissuaded too easily by difficulties, visualising this colour while intoning the name of the angel Samael will increase your capacity for consideration, deliberation and persistence.

Now visualise the colour purple and repeat the name of the angel Zadkiel whose name translates as 'righteousness of God', which can be interpreted as the quality of integrity and nobility. If you feel that you lack a sense of self-worth or your pride has taken a knock, concentrating on this quality of energy will restore your self-respect and self-esteem.

Visualising a violet sphere while intoning the name of the angel Zaphkiel, whose name means 'wisdom of God', will generate a vibration that can stimulate intuition and imagination, improve your concentration and open communication with the higher self. If you suffer from migraine or sinus headaches, visualise a violet sphere in the centre of your forehead and appeal to the angel Zaphkiel. The pressure will ease within minutes.

Now visualise a radiant blue sphere and intone the name of the angel Raziel whose name translates as 'secret of God'. This will enable you to express your thoughts and feelings more readily and enhance your ability to communicate more concisely. It can also benefit on a purely physical level as it can stimulate the antibodies that fight flu and ear infections, soothe sore throats and even regulate an overactive thyroid gland, which controls the metabolism.

Finally, visualise a luminous white sphere while intoning the name of the archangel Metatron, whose name translates as 'spirit of the presence'.

This dissolves fear and generates a tremendous sense of well-being, clarity and serenity and is particularly effective in alleviating depression.

Exercise: Chakra centring

The following exercise is the first significant step in developing an acute awareness of the angelic world and acquiring your own psychic powers. By attuning to the subtle energy of the seven major chakras (which are connecting points between the spirit and the physical body) you will develop greater sensitivity to personal energy and be able to offer healing to others.

Note: For visualisation purposes the Root chakra opens downwards, the Crown opens upwards and the remaining five chakras open front to back.

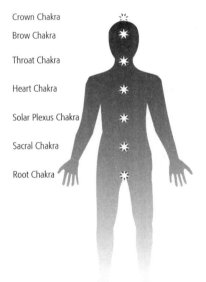

Crown Chakra
Brow Chakra
Throat Chakra
Heart Chakra
Solar Plexus Chakra
Sacral Chakra
Root Chakra

Close your eyes and begin by visualising the rich, brown soil beneath your feet. Sense a tingling in the soles of your feet as the life force rises from the earth into the Root chakra in the perineum at the base of your spine, stimulating the survival instinct and grounding you in the material world. The element associated with this energy centre is Earth, the colour is brown and the associated emotion is stillness. This chakra governs the adrenal glands, the legs, bones and large intestine. Stimulating this chakra can help with obesity, haemorrhoids and constipation.

Now become aware of a tingling sensation in the lower abdomen just below the navel as the Sacral chakra begins to spin, releasing etheric energy concerned with our emotions and sexuality. The element associated with this energy centre is Water, the colour is red and the associated emotion is desire. This chakra governs the ovaries, prostrate and testicles, the womb, kidneys and bladder. Stimulating this chakra can alleviate bladder problems, frigidity and impotence.

Next sense the opening of the Solar Plexus chakra just above the navel. This chakra is concerned with power and the expression of our will. The element associated with this centre is Fire, the colour is yellow and the associated emotions are anger and joy. This chakra governs the pancreas, stomach and muscles. Stimulating it can help treat ulcers, diabetes and hypoglycemia.

The fourth chakra is the Heart chakra, which is located in the centre of the chest. This centre is concerned with compassion. Its element is Air, its colour is green and its associated emotion is unconditional love. This centre governs the thymus, lungs and the heart and stimulating it can help asthma and high blood pressure.

The fifth centre is the Throat chakra, which is concerned with creativity and communication. Its associated element is sound, its colour is blue and the corresponding emotion is excitement and enthusiasm. This centre governs the hypothalamus and the thyroid glands. Stimulating and centring this chakra can help disorders of the throat, ears and mouth.

Now place your palm within an inch (a few centimetres) of the centre of your forehead between the eyebrows. Sense the warmth and the prickly feeling as you stimulate the Third Eye, the organ of psychic sight. Its associated psychological function is imagination, its element is Light, its colour is indigo and its corresponding emotion is dreaming. Working on this Brow chakra can help with eye problems and headaches.

At this point you may even see the Third Eye, which is your own, staring back at you. This can be quite disconcerting if you are not prepared, but there is nothing to be frightened of. Its appearance signals a significant stage in your psychic and spiritual development and it helps you to understand how it is possible for you to be both a physical and a spiritual being, looking out at the world and inward at the same time.

Finally, pass your right palm over the crown of your head and intone the name of the archangel Metatron by whose grace we come to self-realisation. The psychological aspect of the Crown chakra is understanding, its element is thought, its colour is white and its associated emotion is bliss. Allow yourself to be totally absorbed in the spaciousness which this brings and lose all sense of self. Become one with the angels for you are now the stillness at the centre of the universe.

At this moment, in this sacred space and in this state of grace you can ask what you will of the angels and know that your prayer will be answered, your desires will be fulfilled, your path and purpose in life will be revealed and your questions will be answered.

When you are ready, gradually return to waking consciousness by counting slowly down from ten to one and open your eyes.

Giving healing

Once you are attuned to the subtle energy of the chakras and can visualise colours with relative ease, you can offer to heal other people. But before you do so, there are several key points to remember.

- ○ You are not aiming to cure people, although miracles can and do happen. You are offering to alleviate their discomfort if they are in pain and to revitalise them if they feel 'down' or depleted.

- ○ Never make any claims or promises. Your guardian angel is going to help you to be a receptive channel for the universal life force. You are not the source. Never claim credit for the benefits you might help to bring to other people. In many cases you are helping that person to help themselves by stimulating their energy centres, which will then work more efficiently, gathering their own momentum.

- ○ Healers are forbidden from making a diagnosis. You can tell the patient that you feel a cold spot in a certain part of their body, or that you suspect that there might be a blockage in a specific area, but you must always refer them to a qualified medical practitioner if they complain of a chronic condition. You are offering a form of complementary therapy, not medical advice or assistance.

- ○ Healers do not usually charge a fee, but will instead accept a small donation for their chosen charity if it is offered. You could consider this your way of repaying the angels for their help and guidance and, no doubt, your good fortune will increase as a result.

Before treatment

Before the session, work through the grounding (see pages 63–4) and chakra centring visualisations (see pages 79–80), then invite your guardian angel to join you for the benefit of all concerned. The session is not just for the patient. You should also benefit from the infusion of the life force. If you feel exhausted at the end of the session, you are trying too hard.

Ask the client if they have had healing before and if not, put them at their ease by explaining what you are going to do and the fact that they do not have to do anything but relax. Now ask the client to remove their spectacles, if they have any, and their shoes, as this could also be helpful. Then ask them to be seated.

You do not need to touch the patient during treatment, other than during the first few minutes when you place your hands on his or her shoulders to enable you to tune in. This needs to be stated before you begin as some people do not like to be touched by a stranger and it will put the individual at ease to be told that it is not necessary for healing. Healers too can feel self-conscious and uncomfortable if they have to be intimate with a stranger, making them less relaxed and receptive.

During treatment

Do not feel anxious. You are not taking part in a performance. You have nothing to prove. Your compassion for other people will be sufficient to soften your Heart chakra and make you receptive to the healing energy flowing in from your guardian angel.

Do not use your will-power to direct your own energy into another person otherwise you will find yourself exhausted and drained of the vital life force. Relax and be open so that your angel can use you to channel the energy into the patient.

As you stand behind the client, visualise your guardian angel standing behind you. This is crucial as it will attune you to the highest vibrational frequency in the universe and give you the support you will need. As the angel puts its hand on your shoulders you rest your hands on the shoulders of the client. You may feel a detachment from your body and surroundings as the angel raises your vibrational frequency but if you are grounded you will be able to ground this force in much the same way that a lightning rod channels static electricity to Earth.

Once you feel that you have a rapport you can pass the palms of your hands over the client's body at a distance of about an inch (a few centimetres), as you will be conducting the energy in through his or her aura not the skin.

You may feel a tingling or prickly sensation in your hands or you may feel heat emanating from your palms. The client may feel a similar sensation, which should be taken as encouragement as you are obviously getting through to him or her.

When you are ready to move on, begin to scan the client's body from head to toe down the front, back and sides for energy blockages and the source of any symptoms. You may sense these as cold patches indicating poor circulation of etheric energy.

If you see a colour, it is likely to represent the quality of energy that the person needs. In which case, you should visualise radiating that colour from your hands. Otherwise you might stimulate and centre the client's chakras by passing a hand close to each centre and visualising the corresponding colour (see pages 79–80).

After treatment

Make it clear to the client that the treatment has finished by saying something like 'Bless you' or 'I hope that has helped you'. The client then knows that he or she can open his or her eyes.

Let the client sit still for a few moments as it is not unusual for people to feel a little light-headed after healing.

Always ground yourself and wash your hands in cold water after each session, otherwise you risk absorbing disturbances from your patient.

And don't forget to thank your angel for its assistance!

Bear in mind that sometimes (and I must stress sometimes) a patient may manifest symptoms in order to draw attention to an unresolved issue (see 'Self-diagnosis' for examples, pages 72–7). If this is the case you may not be able to bring relief from physical discomfort but you may see a significant symbol or scene while working on the client with your eyes closed. If you see something which you feel may be relevant, then tell the client but do not offer your analysis unless you are a qualified professional therapist.

8

Advanced Angel Techniques

O nce you have explored the various techniques for inviting the angels into your life for healing, protection and guidance, you may want to go further and attain altered states of consciousness in which you can experience the angelic realms for yourself. Or you may wish to connect with the Akashic angels who are said to hold the record of your past lives in order to give meaning to your current personality and circumstances.

If so, the following exercises will provide a safe starting point for the next stage of your inner journey, for it is no longer necessary to renounce the world and become a spiritual recluse, nor to follow in the footsteps of a revered mystic or guru in order to seek the answers to the most profound and fundamental questions. The answers and the teacher are within.

Akashic angels

Most of us have an affinity with a particular place or period in history, but that does not necessarily mean that this is a clue to a past life. If you want to know if your interest in a particular period or place is significant you will need to consult the Akashic records, which is the mystics' term for what Jungian psychologists call the Collective Unconscious.

By connecting with your guardian angel or higher self through the following visualisation you can access this matrix of etheric energy and recover past-life memories which have left an impression in the Universal Mind.

Exercise: Journey into the past

Begin by selecting a piece of music that evokes the place or period that is important to you. Ideally it should be instrumental and ten to twenty minutes in length to provide a soundtrack for your journey into the past. But if a particular song works for you, then use it. Programme your CD player to repeat it, burn a compilation on CD or make a cassette copy so that you have at least ten minutes of background music. If you have a picture to which you can relate, then use that as well.

Put the music on at a low volume and make yourself comfortable. If you have a picture, meditate on it for a couple of minutes before closing your eyes. You will have retained the image in your mind and will now be able to enter the scene and interact with the inhabitants. If you do not have a suitable picture, you can visualise a suitable scene or recall your chosen location while the music plays and do the same once the image is stable in your mind.

If you are having difficulty visualising, you can stimulate your Third Eye by making gentle, circular movements with your index finger in the centre of your forehead until you feel a tickling sensation.

Now ask your guardian angel to draw near and guide you through the regression process. Ask it to reveal any past-life experiences which can shed light on your present personality and circumstances. Ask too for forgiveness for any problems you have caused other people in the past, whether knowingly or unintentionally, so that you can clear any unresolved issues or karmic debt without suffering the same yourself.

Establish a connection with this place and time by working through the five senses one at a time. You are already seeing with the inner eye so now touch the stone of the nearest building or touch the trees and feel the ground under your feet. Next, heighten your sense of smell by taking in the scent of the grass, flowers and the soil. Now raise your awareness of the sounds that surround you and if possible taste something you fancy. If there is nothing suitable, you may be able to taste salt in the air if you are near the sea or the smoke of the city.

Explore wherever you are drawn to. You may find that you can only see ahead of you and that there is a blind spot to either side. If so, go where the image is strong and ask questions continually of your angelic guide. If you do not hear an answer, you may be shown what you seek. And finally, do not be alarmed if you find yourself an observer at your own death. This is a common experience as it was the last significant image you saw in that lifetime. Your death may have been the most significant event in that life and may hold the key to fears and phobias in your present life. But do not be anxious or afraid.

Remember what you are witnessing is merely a replay of past-life memories being rescreened for your benefit.

When you are ready, return to waking consciousness and sit quietly for a few minutes to assimilate the experience.

It is essential that you desensitise yourself after every past-life regression exercise. To do this either visualise closing down the chakras beginning with the Crown, then the Brow chakra, followed by the Throat, Heart, Solar Plexus, Sacral and finally the Root or Base chakra. Then stamp your feet to ground yourself or wash your face and hands in cold water.

Exercise: Exploring past lives

When you are suitably relaxed, visualise yourself standing at the top of a long winding staircase the bottom of which is obscured by a thick rolling mist. Gradually descend the staircase one step at a time and as you do so, you feel more and more relaxed. Down, down you go and as you approach the bottom you notice that there is a luminosity to the mist. It is glowing. There is a soft radiance at the bottom of the staircase and with every step you take this light is growing in intensity.

You pass through the mist and find yourself on solid ground, but you cannot see anything beyond your feet as the mist is too thick. You look down at your feet. What type of footwear do you see? What kind of clothes are you wearing?

The mist begins to clear and you find yourself in the main square of a small town, village or city that you have never visited before, but which is strangely familiar to you. Do not impose any details on the image. Allow it to arise spontaneously. You are not apprehensive but excited at the prospect of exploring this place because there, ahead of you, awaits your guardian angel. Trust it to lead you to somewhere that has some significance for you.

Before setting off to explore, familiarise yourself with your surroundings. What character does the town have? What period does it represent? Are there are signposts which might give you a clue as to where to begin your search? Do you feel drawn in any particular direction or towards a particular building?

When you are ready, begin to explore and be guided by your intuition. Enjoy the tingle of anticipation as you wander at will through a labyrinth of unexplored alleyways and streets anticipating a new discovery at every turn.

Don't impose any expectations upon yourself and don't be disappointed if you don't uncover anything significant on your first outing; enjoy exploring.

Thought forms

One of the most demanding mental disciplines practised by initiates of the various esoteric schools through the centuries is the creation of a thought form. A thought form is a mental image empowered with a life of its own. The Tibetan mystics call them Tulpa creations and kept the technique a closely guarded secret until the 1920s when travel writer and mystic Alexandra David-Neel became the first Western woman to be initiated into their secret doctrines. She was so successful in creating an imaginary figure that it was later seen by her unsuspecting companions who were so unnerved that they demanded that she absorb it back into her body without delay!

There is no danger in creating a thought form of an angel so long as you charge it with a specific task and put a limit on its lifespan. They can be particularly useful if you need protection for your home while you are away or when walking alone at night. Burglars and other undesirables may not see your creation, but as soon as they enter the protected zone they will 'feel' that something is not quite right and go elsewhere. You can also send angelic emissaries to heal friends and relatives when it is not practical for you to visit and you can create a personal angelic bodyguard to accompany a loved one on a long journey.

Exercise: The virtual angel

Begin with the grounding visualisation (see pages 63–4) then centre the seven chakras one at a time (see pages 79–80) until you feel them spinning at an accelerated rate.

When they are all attuned and centred, channel the light from each of the lower chakras (Root, Sacral, Solar Plexus, Heart and Throat) up through the centre of your body into your head. Then draw down the light from the Crown chakra and visualise the life force from these seven energy centres blending together to illuminate you from within. Sense the heat from these seven microcosmic suns radiating the life force until you feel you could overflow with energy.

At this point concentrate the light in a single pulsating sphere in the Third Eye centre between the brows and project it to the other side of the room. Watch as it begins to assume the form of a winged angel armed with a gleaming sword. See it in every detail. The stronger the image you can create and sustain, the more effective your angel will be.

Now give it a clear set of instructions to protect your property or bring healing to someone and a fixed time limit. If you are sending the angel to heal someone, visualise it leaving your home and arriving at the desired location and watch as it carries out its task. Then draw it back and absorb it through your Solar Plexus chakra. If you have empowered it to protect your property, see it towering over the roof of the building and acknowledge it when you awake in the morning and again before you go to sleep at night. When the appointed time comes to end its task, enter a meditative state and visualise drawing your angel back into the room and reabsorbing the energy into your solar plexus.

Then close down the chakras one by one and drink plenty of water and rest for an hour to replenish your energy as this is one of the most demanding exercises of all.

Soul rescuing

Rescuing restless spirits is the highest form of service a psychic can perform, but it is also potentially dangerous and should never be attempted by anyone who is not physically and psychologically sound. Often the soul in question is not disturbed but simply lost. The individual might have died a sudden death in an accident, for example, and not be aware that he or she is no longer in his or her body. In such cases it is the psychic's responsibility to make the individual aware of this fact in as gentle and compassionate a manner as possible, as if waking someone from a deep sleep.

Exercise: Releasing spirits

Soul rescuing is usually performed by four or more individuals who gain strength from the energy generated by the group, but if you decide to practise this process alone you must appeal to your guardian angel for assistance. You need help both on this side and on the other side of life if you are to be successful.

You may have been called to clear a house in which the inhabitants have experienced a disturbance or a chill in the atmosphere, or you may choose to visit the site of a recent accident where you sense there is a lingering presence. In either case, begin by drawing a white circle of light around yourself using visualisation and then appeal to the four archangels for assistance, using the following invocation:

'In the name of Almighty God, creator of all living things I ask for the presence, protection and assistance of my guides and guardian angel. May Raphael go before me, Gabriel behind me, Michael at my right hand and Uriel at my left, while above me shines the six-rayed star, the living presence of God.'

Now close your eyes and ask if there is someone there. You may receive a name or an image. You might have a cold sensation creeping up your body and feel a whirling in the Heart chakra. Once you have made contact, talk to this person as calmly as you would someone who is lost and confused. Reason with the person if they are disturbing the living inhabitants of the house and convince them that they would be better if they went to the light. Ask them if they can see the light which is always there to receive them. Ask too if they have any loved ones who have passed over and, if so, ask the angels to bring that person to collect them.

If they stubbornly refuse to believe that they are no longer alive, encourage them to touch something solid which you can put your hand on. Once they see their hand pass through a solid object the illusion will be broken and they will be willing to walk into the light.

It should be obvious when they have passed over. The atmosphere will change and you may see or hear something to convince you. You may feel a warmth rising from your feet and through your body, and the Heart chakra may spin again or you may experience an overwhelming sensation of relief.

Once you have cleared the area, acknowledge the assistance of the angels and close down in the usual way. It is also beneficial to drink a glass of cold water and take a cool refreshing shower to restore your equilibrium.

9

The Angelic Counsellor

We usually think of angels as the instruments of divine intervention, bringing comfort and reassurance to those in despair, or in rare instances warning of imminent danger. But angels can also serve as an intermediary between people who are in a destructive relationship and those who have issues to resolve. They can also help to bring closure to the bereaved and those suffering any form of loss such as divorce or redundancy. If you are uncomfortable discussing personal issues with a counsellor or therapist, or if you are not ready to do so and you do not wish to burden your friends and family with your problems, you can ask your guardian angel to act as a spiritual counsellor. Whatever issues you have, you can address to the angels in the knowledge that they will always listen, they will not judge you and, most important, their prime concern is your peace of mind. And the great thing about angelic counsellors is that you can turn to them 24 hours a day and each consultation will strengthen your connection.

Exercise: The empty chair

A word of warning: this exercise should not be practised by someone who is suffering from psychological problems or any form of trauma, including recent bereavement.

It is best performed seated.

Make yourself comfortable, close your eyes and establish a regular rhythm of breathing.

Visualise yourself sitting opposite an empty chair. Sustain the image of the empty chair for a few moments before imagining an intense white light hovering an inch (a few centimetres) over the seat.

Now see the light intensify and expand until it takes on the form of a benign, compassionate angelic being. This is your angelic guide and teacher, but you can consider it as your best friend if you prefer, someone you can confide in and with whom you can share your thoughts and feelings without the risk of being judged or contradicted.

Now begin to talk about whatever concerns you at the moment. It can be a difference of opinion that you have had with someone, or what you consider to be an injustice that you have suffered in the past. Feel free to talk openly and express your feelings in the company of the angel who has only your best interests at heart. Perhaps you want to know the reason why something happened to you or someone else? Or maybe you simply want a chance to put your side of the story. Don't feel, just because the other party isn't present, that what you say goes unheard. The angel is listening and it will act as an intermediary between you and the other individual. Even if the other party has passed over to the other side of life, your thoughts and your emotions are carried across regardless of time or distance and will find a resonance. Remember, the primary function of the angels is to convey messages between individuals and between the worlds.

The key to a constructive counselling session is empathy, so see the angel listening, perhaps occasionally nodding and smiling as it acknowledges your concerns. Then listen as it mirrors (repeats) your key words and paraphrases significant sentences in an effort to encourage you to develop that theme and reveal more about a particular attitude, emotion or incident. Listen too as the angel summarises what you have been saying in order to clarify your thoughts and feelings. This is where the real work of the angelic counsellor begins, as it is usually very difficult for us to put aside our sense of hurt, loss or injustice and acknowledge the real source of the problem without the help of an impartial observer.

You will feel considerably better as a result of getting this matter off your chest, so to speak, but it may take more than one 'session' with the angel to clear it completely. Some disputes or ill feeling between individuals has a karmic source (it may have originated in a former life) and therefore it will take a good deal of compassion on your part to forgive and forget. But if you consider that neither of you will be able to move on until you have released each other of this debt then you should see how critical it is for your well-being to let it go. Imagine being bound to this person life after life and with each life the connecting cords becoming stronger, draining the vital force out of each of you as you take it in turns to assert who was right.

Visualise cutting each cord, which connects you chakra to chakra, and watch them shrivel like the dried tendrils of a dead plant. Then see the other person fade from view into the distance and wish them well in life. Know that from this moment on you are truly free from the debilitating bonds that were suffocating both of you.

Angels and self-awareness

We tend to associate angels with appeals for help, comfort and guidance, but they can also be of invaluable assistance in helping us to become more self-aware. In inviting your guardian angel to assist you with exploring your feelings and attitudes you will see how the spiritual and psychological aspects of your psyche converge. Once you understand why you respond to certain situations in the way that you do, you will find it easier to make decisions without your emotions clouding your judgement.

The following exercise can be very revealing, but as with all forms of counselling and psychological therapy it will be of little value unless you put the insights into practice.

Exercise: Angelic attributes

This exercise is ideally performed while seated although it can be done while lying down.

Make yourself comfortable, close your eyes and establish a regular rhythm of breathing.

When you are suitably relaxed, visualise yourself sitting in a pure white cloud looking down on the Earth in the company of your guardian angel. You may see or sense the angel beside you or standing over you, but even if you usually have difficulty visualising, be assured that it is there with you now. Know intuitively that you are not alone but are watched over by the one who has your health and happiness at heart at all times.

From this altitude the air is pure and the world looks beautiful and unspoilt. Everything around you is still and serene and the Earth too looks as if all life has come to a standstill. You are caught in a moment in time with the luxury to reflect on who you truly are with the aid of your guardian angel.

Focus on the phrase 'I have' and what it means to you. It is the first of the seven angelic attributes you can awaken within you. Allow the first impressions to come into your mind without analysing what they might signify. You may want to 'count your blessings' to realise what you have achieved but might not have consciously acknowledged so far. Doing so can bring a sense of satisfaction and purpose to a life that might have appeared to have had no pattern to it previously.

Now consider the phrase 'I feel'. What emotions arise and what do these reveal?

Next contemplate the phrase 'I can'. This is largely concerned with our sense of identity, our sense of purpose and our perception of the world around us. Consider how you express the corresponding qualities of self-will and determination.

The fourth angelic attribute is expressed in the phrase 'I love'. What do you associate with this phrase?

The fifth angelic attribute is expressed in the phrase 'I say'. Contemplate what this phrase reveals about your ability to express yourself and communicate your ideas to others.

The sixth attribute is concerned with insight and intuition. Its energy is expressed in the phrase 'I see' and the ability to visualise and dream. What does the repetition of this phrase reveal?

Finally, repeat the seventh phrase, 'I am'. Contemplating this angelic attribute brings enlightenment and understanding. What images and impressions arise when you repeat this phrase?

When you are ready, return to waking consciousness.

Exercise: Self-analysis

This exercise is ideally performed while lying down.

Relax into a meditative state and when you are calm and centred, begin by visualising yourself lying on a couch in a sparsely furnished white room. There is a statuette of a Buddha in an alcove and freshly cut flowers in blue ceramic vases to either side. The main feature of the room is a large picture window through which you can see a well-tended formal garden with a stream running through the trees and snow-capped mountains in the distance. You appear to be in a remote region far from civilisation – Tibet, perhaps. The sky is azure, the air fresh and invigorating and the sun streams down, gilding the leaves of the plants on the window-sill. Just lying here looking at the view creates a feeling of serenity and a detachment from your worldly concerns.

This consulting room belongs to your celestial psychotherapist to whom you can unburden your anxieties at any time you wish without the inconvenience of having to travel or make an appointment. Better still, it offers its service to you absolutely free of charge. For this first session you are going to indulge in self-analysis. You are going to ask yourself the following questions and allow a sufficient pause at the end of each one to listen for the answer from your inner therapist.

- How would someone else describe your personality? How would someone else see it manifest in your attitude and behaviour?

- Which three adjectives would someone close to you use to describe your less appealing traits? How do you react when you identify these traits in other people? Where might these traits have originated and what advice does your angelic therapist offer to help you deal with them?

○ What have you learnt from people you admired and what have you learnt from those who challenged you? Who did you learn more from?

○ What qualities are you particularly proud of? What talents do you possess? How can you develop these further and to what use can you put them?

○ Which abilities would you like to possess and how can you acquire them?

○ How would someone close to you describe the way you react to problems? Would it be true to say that you rise to the challenge or are you indecisive? Do you deny the problem exists and if you do, does the problem reoccur? Do you blame others for creating a problem? Is it possible that you unconsciously set up a challenging situation in order to face something you fear?

○ Is there something concerning your appearance that makes you uncomfortable and, if so, can you accept it as something that makes you unique? Could it be something that you have been conditioned to see as imperfect by others?

The answers should be self-evident, but if you have difficulties analysing them or resolving the issues raised by this exercise it is recommended that you consult a professional counsellor. It is not advisable to confide such insights to friends and family.

Overcoming nerves

Nervousness, worry and anxiety are symptomatic of a lack of self-confidence, so boost yours by sending your guardian angel in ahead of you the next time you have a job interview, examination or dental appointment. The night before and again five minutes before you go in, visualise your guardian angel walking a few steps in front of you and standing or sitting next to you during the meeting. It is incredible how calm, centred and self-confident you can become when you have a real sense of the angel beside you, rooting for you and, if you listen carefully, giving you the answers you need!

The same solution applies to anger and impatience as you will find it impossible to indulge your temper if you truly believe you are in the presence of an angel, which of course we are every moment of our lives. The trick is to be conscious of the fact.

Facing your fears

'Feel the fear and do it anyway.' (Susan Jeffers)

Fear is a natural human emotion but it is our reaction to the thing we fear that determines the degree to which we intensify the experience. Fear increases physical pain, exacerbates anxiety and elongates the grieving period when we lose someone we love or end a long-term relationship. By walking through your fear in the company of your guardian angel you can face your phobia at a safe distance in a visualisation and perhaps reveal the source of your anxiety.

Visualise yourself in the company of your guardian angel facing your fear together in easy stages. If, for example, you have a fear of snakes, visualise being taken in hand by your angel to look into a glass reptile aquarium which houses one tiny baby snake the size of the smallest worm. The snake is harmless and more frightened of you than you are of it. It cannot climb out of the aquarium. Your angel reaches in and calms it, for it fears what it must perceive as a giant predator – you. Can you truthfully say that you are frightened of snakes in such circumstances? Listen to your guardian angel who will tell you that it is not the snake you are frightened of, but something the snake symbolises. Ask your angel what it is that the snake symbolises for you.

Be prepared to practise this exercise periodically and probe gently. However, once the origin of the phobia has been identified the focus of your phobia will lose its power to frighten.

Resolving conflict

If you have a disagreement or difficult relationship with someone and find it hard to talk it through with them, you can resolve the issue by eliciting the help of your guardian angel who will intervene on your behalf. After all, angels are there to establish harmony in the universe and if you are willing to accept that the other person might have an equally valid point of view, there is no reason why conflict cannot be resolved on a spiritual plane. If you find it difficult to believe such things are possible, then feel free to consider it instead a meeting of minds on some more subtle level. But give it a try, because it works!

Visualise yourself seated opposite the person with whom you have the disagreement. See your angel and theirs in the middle acting as arbitrators. Visualise them listening dispassionately as you both put your side of the argument. Then ask that it be resolved for the highest good of all concerned and think no more about it. But be prepared for a change in the other party's attitude toward you the next time you meet.

Goal setting

You cannot hope to attain something until you have identified exactly what it is that you want and have impressed that desire in the unconscious.

Each day choose one short-term goal from the following categories and work through the appropriate meditation while asking your guardian angel to help you find your true path to your true place so that your potential may be fulfilled.

Personal qualities

Having identified the qualities you need, visualise yourself exhibiting those qualities in an appropriate setting and being appreciated for your efforts. For example, if you wish you had more patience, see yourself looking calm and relaxed while someone else becomes flustered and ill tempered. See yourself remaining still in the centre of this storm of emotion and affirm that you do not want to act like this person because he or she is alienating everyone nearby and heading for a heart attack or stroke.

Alternatively, you could imagine listening to a young child (preferably your own) who is eager to tell you a story in great detail. They continually pause to recall significant details and struggle for the right words, but you listen with great patience and resist the temptation to interrupt because it is important to the child that you hear the whole story. Affirm that in the future you will, where possible, treat everyone as patiently as you have that child.

Career

If you want to progress in your current job or find a more satisfying career then simply visualise a typical day in that ideal job. Trace every move you make from waking in the morning to coming home in the evening.

Money

If you want to be more prosperous you need to affirm that the universe has an abundance of everything and that you are entitled to your share. Write a similar statement in your own words and repeat it three times in the morning, again in the afternoon and, finally, before you go to sleep at night. As you say it, visualise yourself enjoying a prosperous lifestyle.

Lifestyle

Again, the most effective way of acquiring a more leisurely lifestyle is to visualise it whilst affirming that you have earned it.

Relationships

If you wish to find a new partner, visualise your ideal scene. It could be a family holiday or a romantic evening but, whatever the setting, it is important not to impose any detail on your partner. Affirm that you will accept whoever the angels send and is right for you. That does not, of course, mean that you should feel obliged to commit to the first person who shows an interest in you. What it means is that you declare yourself willing to see the best in each potential partner and to make the best of it until you can be certain one way or the other. If you insist on a specific type or characteristic you risk attracting someone who appears promising but who may ultimately prove unsuitable.

Self-expression

Free the creativity angel by enjoying the satisfaction that comes from spontaneous self-expression.

It is not a fanciful notion but a fact that we are divine beings brimming with creative potential. But it is also a fact that many of us belittle our talents and limit our power for self-expression either because we are afraid of failure or, paradoxically, because we are afraid of success.

Whatever form your creativity takes, you need to see it as a release, as something to play with rather than something to work at. Whether you cook, compose music, practise a physical discipline or craft something with your hands, it will never rise above a learnt skill unless you lose yourself in it and let your higher self take over. Once you reach this state, being creative becomes as effortless and natural as riding a bike.

If you have the urge to be creative, but lack the motivation or inspiration, relax into a meditative state and ask your guardian angel these questions:

- What attracted me to X?

- What did I hope to achieve?

- What would I feel if I succeeded at X?

- Why did I stop X?

- What am I trying to achieve with X?

- What do I feel when I do X?

- Can I do X even if my talent is not recognised?

- Do I feel obliged to produce something significant or of value?

- Am I doing this for myself or to impress someone else?

○ What positive comments have people made about what I do and how did that make me feel?

Finally, put yourself in the place of your guardian angel and watch your physical self performing whatever creative activity you enjoy. See yourself as your angel sees you. Observe yourself with detachment and ask how you can improve your performance or skill. Are you moving effortlessly, or are you exercising too much effort? Are you working efficiently or forcing your will on the task in hand?

If you have been frustrated in your ambition to succeed, don't repress your anger. Acknowledge it and use that energy. Anger is not negative unless we channel it for a destructive purpose. If you can use your anger to generate ambition and the will to show those doubters what you are capable of, then it will not be wasted.

Once you are motivated and have identified what you really want to do, visualise yourself perfecting your art, executing your finest performance or presenting your work to your guardian angel as a gift for all it has done for you. Sense the pleasure you give in realising something which you were born to do. No one has the right to take that away from you. You are not obliged to offer it for public appraisal if you choose not to do so. It wasn't given to you to make money or to draw acclaim. If it brings these bonuses and they give you pleasure, then you can be sure that your guardian angel is enjoying the sense of satisfaction and the happiness that you give to others too. If not, then indulge your creative urge for the pleasure it gives you and your guardian angel alone.

Personal growth

Write the following affirmation or one of your own choosing in your angel journal and repeat it like a mantra three times in the morning, again in the afternoon and, finally, before you go to sleep. 'I am perfect and complete in myself. I am open to receive whatever experience will increase my self-awareness and the realisation of my full potential.'

Then take a practical step towards increasing your knowledge of the world or of yourself by enrolling in an evening class or distance-learning course of your choosing.

Angel cards

You can make your own angel cards for divination and meditation by obtaining a sheet of thick card from an art shop and using an ordinary playing card as a template. Some stationery suppliers and small printers will even cut the cards for you for a nominal charge and round the edges, making them easier to handle. Remember to ask for card with a gloss finish and not matt as cards made with the latter are likely to stick together when you shuffle them.

Once you have your blank deck you can illustrate them yourself, thereby infusing them with your personal energy, or you can stick on suitable pictures from magazines. But don't forget to write the name of the angel at the top or bottom of the picture and make a copy of the 'key to the cards' (see pages 100–104) so that you can refer to it until you are sufficiently familiar with the interpretations.

If you want to test the effectiveness of the cards before committing yourself, all you need do is write the name of an angel on each card. I guarantee you will want to express your creativity once you've tried them. You may even find that a personal hand-made deck is the perfect gift for friends!

How they work

Each of the angels personifies a theme derived from the pictographic meaning of a letter of the Hebrew alphabet. Each letter is understood to have a mystical significance. Unlike conventional tarot cards, angel cards provide a psychological and spiritual profile of the person consulting the cards to explain why they are encountering particular problems, what lessons these are trying to teach that person and how they can use them for greater self-awareness and spiritual growth.

Although they can be used for divination, the cards reveal that the future is not the result of random events, but determined by the choices we make given our current circumstances and personality. For it is my understanding that the exercising of an individual's free will determines their destiny, not fate.

Each of the 22 cards has four levels of meaning corresponding to the four dimensions in which we have our existence.

○ The words and phrases relating to the physical world will indicate what action needs to be taken in the current circumstances.

○ The words or phrases relating to the emotional realm can reveal the emotional root of a problem or identify the emotional quality needed to overcome a difficulty.

○ The words or phrases relating to the mental level present the intellectual attributes that are required to resolve the situation successfully.

○ The words or phrases indicated at the spiritual level can reveal the purpose and meaning behind a situation. This is indicated by the main theme of the card, such as 'steady labour' or 'structure and form', which for the purpose of the cards has been attributed to a specific angel.

You will see that the main theme resonates down through the other levels so that both obstacles and opportunities provide a learning opportunity for us on a spiritual, mental, emotional and practical level.

Key to the cards

The angel of	Symbol	Mental attributes	Emotional qualities	Form of action
Steady labour	An ox	Tenacity, patience, determination and drive. The cultivation of new ideas.	The need to clear blockages, dispel negative conditioning, overcome self-defeating attitudes and kick old habits.	A time to clear the ground for new projects.
Structure and form	A house	The need to be practical.	Bringing opposing forces into balance, creating harmony and a sense of security. The desire for form and structure.	Establishing a firm foundation, order and stability.
Self-discovery	A camel	Accepting responsibility, a sense of duty, tolerance.	Devotion and loyalty.	An act of selfless service.
Opportunity	An open door	Careful consideration and a willingness to face the truth.	The courage to change.	Transition offering new insights, knowledge and experience.
Objectivity	A window	Vision (seeing the bigger picture). The need for a balanced perspective.	Impartiality.	Gathering, sifting and assimilating the facts to perceive the truth of a situation.

The angel of	Symbol	Mental attributes	Emotional qualities	Form of action
Decisiveness	A nail	Reasoning, distillation of energy to a specific point and purpose.	Toughness and resilience.	To join, to bring together and secure; to bring something to a conclusion.
Justice	A sword	Self-confidence. Taking a fair and balanced view of a situation. Considering the opinion of others. Understanding that there are two sides to truth.	Restraint, constancy and fortitude.	The need to take decisive action to resolve a situation whilst accepting the fact that there may be more than one 'right' way.
Restriction	A wall or fence	Wariness, the instinct for self-preservation, the need for personal space.	Self-containment, a sense of insecurity and a reluctance to give of oneself for fear of being hurt or disappointed, the need to trust others and life.	A barrier to progress to be overcome and a time to face imagined fears and doubts. A boundary to be crossed or to be respected (possibly a self-imposed limitation).
Caution	A serpent	Vigilance. Be wary of self-defeating tendencies that could undermine your efforts, and keep your objective in sight.	Resourcefulness.	A time to cast off what no longer has value or use.

The angel of	Symbol	Mental attributes	Emotional qualities	Form of action
Compromise	A hand	The importance of trust.	The need for agreement or reconciliation. The bestowing of strength or a blessing.	Making a commitment.
Prosperity	An open palm	The need to cultivate a sense of self-worth and to be open to a higher influence.	Importance of being able to give and receive graciously. A sense of well-being and fulfilment. Abundance.	Acting in faith, knowing that the means will be provided.
New directions and action	An ox goad or stick	A willingness to explore and make the most of opportunities	The need to overcome stubbornness or indecision.	Directing your expertise and knowledge to inspire others or allowing others to learn from their own 'mistakes'. A spur to action.
Adaptability	Water	Clear thinking, a willingness to compromise, diplomacy.	Easygoing, the need to accept life as you find it, being flexible and versatile, adapting to circumstances.	Letting go, making the best of a situation. Overcoming obstacles.
Harmony	A fish	Being open to ideas, the need to be directed to an end.	Contentment, sincerity (being honest with oneself).	Time to go with the flow but not be swept along aimlessly by the current.

The angel of	Symbol	Mental attributes	Emotional qualities	Form of action
Virtue	A prop or support	Self-discipline, self-sufficiency.	The need to keep emotions under control.	The need to act in faith, knowing that unseen forces are assisting from the other side.
Insight	An eye	Foresight, self-awareness.	An aspiration for greater insight and understanding which needs to be balanced with dispassionate analysis.	Soul-searching, active self-analysis.
Communication	A mouth	The ability to communicate ideas clearly and concisely; the importance of finding the right words.	The ability to express feelings without becoming emotional.	A time for self-expression and clear communication in order to convince others of the truth of what you believe.
Compliance	A fish hook	Faith and the willingness to entrust your well-being to the influence of the higher self.	Ability to accept the current circumstances and conditions. But also a tendency to let emotions cloud your judgement or to be unduly influenced by others.	Withdrawal. Biding one's time. Preserving strength for another day.
The unconscious	Back of head	Imagination, increasing intuition, inspiration and idealism.	Self-esteem and self-respect. The need to take pride in your achievements.	The need to act on impulse.

The angel of	Symbol	Mental attributes	Emotional qualities	Form of action
Discrimination and discernment	Front of head	Reason, logical thinking and common sense.	Having the courage of your convictions.	A time to make rational, informed choices and, having made them, remain firm.
Self-determination	A tooth	Resolve and a sense of purpose.	Fortitude, firmness in the face of difficulties or resistance.	Hard, prolonged work, grinding down resistance.
Innovation	A mark or cross	Acceptance of new ideas.	Inquisitiveness, a sense of adventure.	Returning to a source of strength or the inception of something significant. A new beginning.

Consulting the cards

When you are looking for direct inspiration or guidance and you do not have a specific question to ask, just shuffle the cards and then choose one at random. You can pick a card from the top or spread them in a fan shape and select one using intuition.

Then turn it face up and consider its significance in the light of your current circumstances. The more familiar you become with the cards and the interpretations, the more you will see in them and the greater insights you will glean.

Using the cards to develop psychic awareness

If you can find three or more willing friends you can use the cards to increase your psychic sensitivity and develop an ability known as psychometry, which involves gathering psychic impressions from personal objects.

Ask the participants to sit in a circle then shuffle the cards and present them face down in a fan shape to each person in turn. Each person should pick a card, look at it and hold it for a few moments. When everyone has a card, put the remainder of the deck to one side. Then collect the cards that have been chosen and put them face down in a pile of their own. Now ask each person to pick one of these cards without looking at it. If they have chosen their own card they must return it and take another.

When each person has a card, they take it in turn to tune into that card and tell the group who they feel it belonged to and anything else about the card or that person that they can glean from the card.

It is important that no one responds 'yes' or 'no' at this point as this could influence those who have yet to 'guess' who their card originally belonged to.

I have practised this exercise with a group of five highly developed psychics and can honestly say that not only did we all 'guess' correctly who the card had belonged to, but we also picked up revealing insights into that person and their recent activities.

Two sample spreads

Two simple spreads are described in the following pages and a sample 'reading' given so that you can work confidently with the deck from day one. Once you become familiar with the images there should be less need for you to refer to the key to the cards. From then on you will find the images take on a life and significance of their own as you begin to use them as a focus for your own psychic sensitivity and intuition.

Note: Unlike the tarot cards, there is no reverse or negative meaning in the angel cards and therefore no significance is to be attached to a card that is dealt upside down. In the event that a card appears upside down, simply place it the right way up and continue the reading.

THE THREE-CARD SPREAD FOR GUIDANCE

Shuffle the cards thoroughly while repeating the question to which you seek an answer. The question should be concise and unambiguous. 'Is it right for me to accept Mr Smith's offer of a job?' is more likely to produce a definitive answer than 'Should I give up work and look for something better?'

If you wish to read the cards for someone else, that person should shuffle the cards while asking the question in his or her mind before handing the cards back to you to lay out in the order indicated. It is better if the person does not reveal the question to you until after you have given the reading.

Take three cards from the top and place them face up in front of you from left to right.

Select the words from the 'Key to the cards' that are relevant to your question and trust your first impressions. Do not be tempted to get too deeply into the significance of the individual symbols.

Consider all three cards to give the complete picture, but be aware that there may not always be a definitive answer. There may be positive aspects to both options. Or one card might act to qualify the answer suggesting, for example, that you will need to overcome your self-doubt if you are to succeed.

THE SEVEN-CARD SPREAD (PAST, PRESENT AND FUTURE)

Enter a relaxed, meditative state by focusing on the breath and ask for inner guidance in words of your own choosing.

Shuffle the cards thoroughly then lay the top seven cards face down from left to right as indicated.

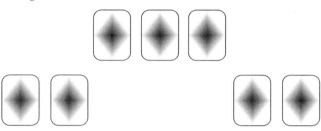

Turn one card over at a time starting from the left. Meditate on its meaning and record your thoughts on paper before turning over the next card.

The first two cards indicate influences in your life from the recent past (the past three to six months), the third, fourth and fifth cards relate to your present circumstances and the last two indicate possibilities in the immediate future (the next three to six months).

Sample reading

During the period in which I developed these cards I drew the following cards for a client:

RECENT PAST The angel of discrimination and discernment (front of head). This card indicates that during the past three to six months the lady concerned needed to be practical and use her discrimination and discernment to sort what was important for her from what no longer had any value. It was a time for her to discard things, places and even people that she might have been clinging to for purely sentimental reasons. On a mental level she had to be logical and use her reason and common sense to make important decisions and not let her emotions affect her judgement. Emotionally, she needed to have the courage of her convictions to make rational, informed choices and, having made them, remain firm.

RECENT PAST The angel of communication (mouth). The theme of this card is self-expression and clear communication. In the last few months she had to communicate her ideas clearly and concisely and not assume that other people understood her feelings, needs and point of view because of the visual signs that she had given them. There might have been occasions when there were misunderstandings and friction because she had not made herself clear to other people. Or perhaps she hadn't been direct enough because she didn't want to hurt their feelings. She will now need to be more explicit if she wants to be understood.

The other theme of this card highlighted her need to be able to express her feelings without becoming emotional. Perhaps in the recent past she had been unable to make important decisions because she let sentiment or concern for other people's feelings prevent her from making significant changes in her life. And on a practical level she needed to express her ideas and feelings effectively in order to convince others of the truth of what she believed. This quality will prove to be important in her future too.

PRESENT The angel of innovation (mark). The main theme of this card is a beginning or a return. She may now find herself returning to something or someone that had been a source of strength in the past and using it or them to make a new start. On a mental level this will require her to be receptive to new ideas and on an emotional level she will need to be inquisitive and demonstrate a sense of adventure. This is a very important card as it indicates that now is the time for something new and significant in her life.

PRESENT The angel of self-discovery (camel). This card refers to the means by which she is journeying to self-discovery. What that is, only she can know, but it is something she is doing at present that gives her insight and understanding. The card is affirming that it is the right path for her and that she should pursue this direction even though progress may be perceived to be slow. On a mental level she now needs to exhibit a sense of duty, responsibility and tolerance towards what she perceives to be other people's failings. Emotionally she will be required to demonstrate devotion and loyalty and on a practical level it could involve an act of selfless service such as caring for an elderly relative or giving freely of her time to help others.

PRESENT The angel of compliance (fish hook). Despite this theme of security there is an element in her life that is in some way unresolved. Either she has a tendency to indecision or someone or something is pulling her in a direction that she feels is not the way she wants to go. To overcome this nagging doubt she will need to have faith in a positive outcome (that her guardian angel has her well-being and best interests at heart and will guide her along her true path to her right place if she will allow it). She does not need to rationalise everything because in doing so she risks dismissing that still small voice within. If she can learn to trust her intuition and occasionally act on impulse (within reason) she may be pleasantly surprised where she ends up.

The fish hook can also indicate a person who allows their emotions to cloud their judgement (a recurring theme in this reading), or someone who can be unduly influenced by others, so she should be aware of this tendency if she feels that this is true for her.

IMMEDIATE FUTURE The angel of decisiveness (nail). The main theme of this card is the distillation of energy to a specific point and purpose. This indicates that in the next three to six months she will be concentrating all her energy into a particular task, making herself secure and committing herself to one place, activity or person after being unsettled.

On a mental level this will manifest as the quality of reasoning and decisiveness and on an emotional level as toughness and resilience. These are the qualities that she will need to carry her through to the next phase of her life. On a practical level she will finally be bringing something to a conclusion, joining something (a group, workplace or institution) and in doing so securing her future happiness.

IMMEDIATE FUTURE The angel of objectivity (window). The main theme of this card is the need for a balanced perspective. So, the next three to six months should be a time to settle and take stock with the understanding that there are two sides to every situation to be considered. She needs to have vision, to see the bigger picture and not just her own point of view. Emotionally she will need to be objective and impartial in any dispute. The form of action that is indicated by this card is gathering, sifting and assimilating the facts to perceive the truth of a situation and, again, not allowing her emotions to cloud her judgement.

Altogether this was a positive reading with a note or two of caution and some revealing insights into her character, which she confirmed.

10

Angel Magic

'Magic is the art of producing changes of consciousness in accordance with the Will.' (Dion Fortune)

Contrary to popular belief, modern ritual magic is not an archaic pagan practice concerned with conjuring spirits and repeating incantations from dusty old grimoires. It is a largely psychological process using symbols, sigils and spells to align the magus with the elements of the universe which correspond to aspects of his or her own psyche. It is no longer necessary for practitioners to perform ceremonies attired in flamboyant robes or to make grand, theatrical gestures before an altar adorned with occult paraphernalia. Today the majority of magicians, both male and female, prefer to perform their rituals as visualisations creating a temple on the inner plane where the real transformations take place.

The following exercise uses the symbols of traditional ceremonial magic to facilitate an altered state of consciousness in which you can connect with the four archangels.

Exercise: Invocation of the archangels

Make yourself comfortable and enter a state of deep relaxation.

When you are ready, visualise yourself in the inner chamber of a temple illuminated by flaming torches, one on each of the four walls. The floor is composed of black and white tiles symbolising the unity of the two complementary aspects at work in the universe which are expressed in our physical world as active and passive, positive and negative, male and female.

To your right is the door to the South covered by a red curtain embroidered with a rod or staff, symbol of Fire. Red represents the Midday sun while the direction denotes the Summer.

To your left is the North door sealed by a green curtain embroidered with a pentacle at the centre of a shield symbolising the Earth. In this context green represents Midnight while the direction denotes Winter.

Behind you is the door of the West obscured by a blue curtain embroidered with a chalice, symbol of Water. Blue represents the setting sun of Evening while the direction denotes Autumn.

Facing you is the door to the East obscured by a yellow curtain embroidered with a sword which is the symbol of the element of Air. The colour of the curtain represents the rising sun of Morning while the direction denotes the Spring.

You acknowledge each of these four cardinal points in turn and the elements they represent. Consider how each represents an aspect of yourself, the four ages from birth to death, the four physical elements within and the four levels of consciousness. You are the universe in miniature. You contain all that exists in finite form.

You now stand before an altar in the centre of the temple framed by two pillars, one of pure white marble and the other of black onyx. They represent the principles of Form and Force, which give dynamic to the universe, while you, standing between them, represent the pillar of Equilibrium which brings these opposing principles into balance.

On the altar stand two candles in candle holders. What colour are the candles? You light them and place something on the altar. It is an offering you have brought with you from the outside world. What offering did you bring?

You are now ready to invoke the archangels. See yourself standing or kneeling before the altar with your arms outstretched as you make the following invocation:

'Before me Raphael, behind me Gabriel, by my right hand Michael, by my left hand Uriel and above me shines the Shekhinah, the divine presence.'

See the four coloured curtains billowing as the doors open and the temple is flooded with light. You avert your eyes and a moment later when you look again you are in the presence of the four archangels who stand towering over you. You cannot look upon their faces, for the light of their presence is intense, though not blinding. In their radiance you glimpse a greater reality. They now surround you and you are overwhelmed by a sense of the Divine.

You are at the centre of a divine energy field generated by the archangels. Sense yourself becoming detached from your body and rising upward towards the ceiling, releasing all suppressed emotions and all sense of guilt, resentment, regret and anger. You are purged of these emotions which have no reality in this place. Such thoughts and feelings fall away from you as readily as discarded clothes, leaving you with a feeling of liberation and of having been cleansed to the very core of your being.

In this state of heightened awareness you realise that although each of the four archangels is a discarnate entity, it is also a personification of an aspect of your own psyche. In the same way that you and your higher self are separate and also one and the same. You have the illusion of a separate existence and yet you are an indivisible element of all that exists, a cell in the body of a greater being, a beautiful thought in the mind of the Divine.

A moment later, the archangels withdraw and you find yourself alone in the temple with the flickering light of the torches burnishing the walls. Have they left a gift for you on the altar? If so, it could be an object whose significance will become evident later or it could be a written message on parchment or in a book. Whatever it is, take it with you as you depart. Give thanks to the archangels and withdraw. Return to normal consciousness by counting down from ten to one and, as you do so, gradually become aware once again of your surroundings and open your eyes.

'We do not affect fate by our magical operations, we affect ourselves; we reinforce those aspects of our nature which are in sympathy with the powers we invoke.' (Dion Fortune)

11

Angels and Kabbalah

I f you are serious in your search for greater self-knowledge and you wish to attain heightened states of awareness of the angelic realms, you will need a basic understanding of the principles of Kabbalah.

Kabbalah is the ancient Jewish metaphysical philosophy which seeks to explain our place and purpose in existence through a symbolic diagram known as the Tree of Life (see below). By exploring the ten spheres (or sephirah) on the Tree in a guided visualisation (see 'Exercise: House of angels', pages 113–18) you can interact with the angels who personify these divine attributes, which are also manifest in yourself.

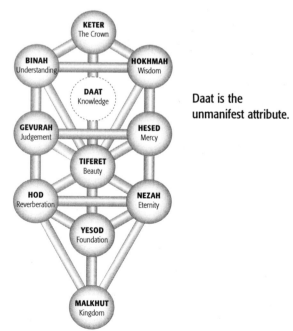

Daat is the
unmanifest attribute.

Note: It is recommended that you record the script or ask a friend to read it while you visualise. Allow pauses at suitable places so that you have time to take in the details of your surroundings and absorb the atmosphere. With practice you will become sufficiently familiar with the process to be able to recall the details without assistance.

Exercise: House of angels

When you are fully relaxed, visualise yourself standing outside a building whose appearance, size, décor and state of repair will be symbolic of your current state of mind. This image should appear spontaneously. Do not be tempted to manipulate the image in any way or impose features upon it in order to fulfil your expectation of what you think you ought to see. You may have expected or wished to see something exotic such as an Egyptian pyramid, an ancient temple or a manor house, but if a cottage or modern house appears, accept it. Its significance will become apparent in due course.

Observe as much detail as you can, but do not be tempted to analyse anything until after you return to waking consciousness.

Sandalphon, the angel of Malkhut (the kingdom/ the Earth)

You enter the grounds of the building where you find Sandalphon attired in russet brown robes and with wings of a darkened hue signifying its connection to the physical world. It will greet you and introduce you to a strong-looking young man or woman who is the archetype of this sphere. He or she will ask what plans you have for the garden. The archetype will create the garden and cultivate the plants and trees, but you have to give him or her an outline of your plans. What decisions do you make? How do you envisage your ideal garden sanctuary? Do you want a formal or informal garden? What state is the garden in now? What work needs doing?

As you survey the grounds in the company of the angel and the archetype you become aware that the human body is a microcosm, a world in miniature containing all the elements that exist in Nature and in the universe (the macrocosm). The element of Earth is represented by the solidity of your bones, the element of Water by the fluidity of your blood, the element of Air by your breath and the element of Fire by the heat in your skin.

Now consider the mineral element in your bones that appear solid but are continually growing and the basic minerals that maintain the vital chemical balance in the body. Then consider the vegetable principle which governs growth and regeneration of the cells. Now become aware of the animal principle – your vitality, curiosity, instinct, sociability and mobility. Finally, become aware of your human attributes – your imagination, inventiveness, memory, reflection and your ability to expand your consciousness and awareness. And finally, your free will – the facility to create your own reality according to your will. If you want to change anything in your life you first have to visualise your ideal scene, then empower it with your desire and determination to see it brought into being. Finally, you have to act in faith in expectation of your wish coming to pass. In short, you have to meet the angels halfway so that they can provide the means to make your desires a reality.

Gabriel, the angel of Yesod (the foundation/ the inner child)

You now enter the entrance hall of the main building where you will find Gabriel, the angel of Yesod whose robes and wings are red, the primary colour corresponding to this divine aspect of your psyche. It introduces you to the archetype of this level, which is a child. The child takes delight in showing off an entire town that it has constructed from multi-coloured building blocks, but when you look as if you're losing interest, it destroys it in an attempt to win back your attention. How do you react? Do you have the patience to help it to put it all back together again? Can you relate to the archetype who personifies your inner child or ego?

An alternative scenario is to visualise the archetype in the form of an ambitious and vain young man who acts as your guide around the lower levels of the building. In each room he covets every object he shows you and boasts of the cunning means by which he acquired them. Again, what is your response?

Raphael, the angel of Hod (reverberation/the intellect)

Now enter the first room on your left. It is a library in which you will find Raphael, the angel of Hod in fiery yellow robes and with wings of the same colour. It introduces you to the archetype of this level, which is in the form of an enthusiastic young student who is eager to learn whatever you can tell of the outside world. Hod is the aspect of your psyche concerned with the intellect.

You engage in a discussion that draws on your practical knowledge of how things work and on the archetype's theoretical knowledge. Let its enthusiasm inspire you. If there is something that you have always wanted to learn about, take encouragement from what you find here. Everything you have always wanted to know is waiting to be discovered. Everything that you have learnt and experienced has left its indelible impression in the mind. You only have to enter this library to recollect it.

Uriel, the angel of Nezah (eternity/instinct)

You leave the library through a door which leads you into the grounds at the rear of the building. It is a pleasure garden with long tree-lined walks, ornamental fountains, statues and an elaborate maze. Do you risk losing yourself in the maze, and if so, what do you find there?

You explore the grounds, sniffing each scented rose bush and savouring the smell of freshly cut grass. Now stroll into the orchard and pick a peach from a tree laden with ripe fruit. Feel the texture of the peach as you turn it over in your hand before biting into its juicy flesh. When you have satisfied your appetite you find that your attention is drawn to another part of the garden where you can hear the faint strains of beautiful music mingling with the sound of bubbling water in the fountains and the sweet chirping of birdsong. Enter this secluded part of the grounds and indulge yourself in the pleasures on offer. You might find yourself at a grand picnic with music and dancing, or invited to join in frivolous games presided over by the angel of Nezah robed in orange with almost translucent wings. This is the area of the psyche in which you can explore your sensuality, impulses and instincts presided over by the archetype of this level, a sensual figure of indeterminate gender.

Michael, the angel of Tiferet (beauty)

You leave the pleasure garden and wander through the grounds until you come to a secluded walled garden whose entrance is hidden behind vines and overgrown weeds. This is your inner sanctuary, your own personal sacred space offering you peace of mind, serenity and a sense of security. Here you meet and ask for guidance from the Archangel Michael who is robed in green. His wings are of burnished gold and he presents you with a symbolic gift, the significance of which reveal itself if not now, then later. Know that whatever form the archetype of this level takes, it is an aspect of your own personality and that you have this all-knowing supreme being within you to call upon at any time you choose.

Samael, the angel of Gevurah (judgement)

When you are ready to return to the main building you enter through a side door and find yourself in a chamber presided over by the Samael, the angel of judgement. The predominant colour of this angel is indigo. It introduces you to the archetype of this level, which can take the form of a judge or inquisitor armed with a book of the law. It personifies the qualities of restraint, discernment and discrimination, but if its judgements are not tempered with mercy and compassion it can lead you to become self-critical and to become someone who finds fault in everything and everyone.

Visualise this archetype weighing the evidence in a case that is strikingly similar to one that occupies you at the moment in the 'real world'. You view the evidence and hear the arguments from both sides with impartiality then retire to the solitude of a side room to contemplate the verdict. Can you now see a way to resolve a conflict that you have with someone? Perhaps you now see that a dispute is the result of a misunderstanding or your failure to appreciate the other person's point of view.

Zadkiel, the angel of Hesed (mercy)

Leave the chamber of judgement and cross the passage. Enter the room directly opposite where you will meet Zadkiel, the angel of Hesed robed in purple and with wings of the same colour. It introduces you to the archetype of this level in the form of a maternal figure who offers unconditional love, compassion and commitment to your well-being. In her company you can unburden yourself of any feelings of guilt, anger, envy or whatever needs to be cleared in the certainty that you will be forgiven.

Come as a child and remember how acutely you felt every injustice and harsh word at that time of your life. Affirm that you will treat every individual you meet from now on with compassion, as someone who is still learning through experience, and resolve to be as forgiving of your own mistakes.

Zaphkiel, the angel of Binah (understanding)

Now pass through Tiferet on up to a second chamber on the first floor where you meet Zaphkiel, the angel of Binah robed in violet with wings of electric blue. It introduces you to the archetype of this level, which takes the form of an erudite specialist in a subject that interests you. It could be an academic, a scientist, a skilled craftsman, a qualified professional, or a medical professional. Visit it in its natural environment and sense the tradition of knowledge, training, understanding and skill that lies behind its expertise. What do you ask it? What is its response? Do you have an aspiration that is unfulfilled? If so, how does it advise you to overcome the obstacles and fulfil that potential? The archetype is the personification of reason and understanding. It is accessible to you at all times to reveal the underlying reason behind the events that occur in your life.

Raziel, the angel of Hokhmah (wisdom)

Opposite Binah is the chamber presided over by Raziel, the angel of Hokhmah, robed in blue with wings of the same colour. It introduces you to the archetype of this level, which takes the form of a guru, philosopher or spiritual teacher. You are honoured with a private audience in a setting that lends itself to quiet reflection. Become aware of the aura of stillness and serenity that emanates from the presence of the teacher as your questions are answered with infinite patience. After some time you are overwhelmed by the teacher's unconditional love for humanity and generosity of spirit and find yourself becoming one with your teacher. You look out through the eyes of the teacher and perceive the greater reality that lies beyond the physical world. You are now acutely aware of the unity of all things and your place and purpose in existence.

Metatron, the angel of Keter (the crown/divine will)

You are now in a state of deep relaxation and heightened awareness. You have no sense of the solidity of your body and are oblivious to your surroundings. You find yourself rising into the air and out through the roof of the building into the night sky. You are as light as a bubble.

Float up above the clouds and observe the teeming variety of life below. See the villages, towns and cities and their inhabitants contributing their experience of life to the group soul. See the hosts of angels watching over the newly born, the young, the middle aged, the elderly and those who are ready to return to the realm of spirit.

Look down on the turning world, nourished by the blue waters of the oceans, rivers, lakes and streams and by the warmth of the sun. Know that the Earth is a sentient being, a living planet capable of regenerating and sustaining itself and affirm that no matter how badly human kind pollutes and abuses it, life will continue in one form or another. The life force is stronger than any contrary destructive impulse. The nature spirits and the angels will ensure the divine will manifests in many forms. You do not need to worry or fear for the future. Your part is to enjoy and experience that which was created by you and for you, in love and in peace.

You are in the presence of Metatron, the supreme being who resides immediately below the throne of God. According to biblical mythology, Metatron was once a human being, Enoch, the first man to attain enlightenment, who was then taken up to heaven without 'tasting death' and transformed into the supreme archangel. Such stories suggest that we may all be angels in the making.

When you are ready, return to waking consciousness.

Note: After having familiarised yourself with the divine attributes as they are arranged on the Tree of Life you can then choose to explore one or more in subsequent visualisations to study the relationship between them, in pairs or a triad. Begin the visualisation as described, and when the image of the building is stable simply go to the room that is symbolic of the divine attribute you have chosen to examine.

Contemplate:
- Sandalphon, the angel of the Earth (Malkhut), if you need to be more practical and grounded.

○ Gabriel, the angel of the inner child (Yesod), if you want to understand your perception of the world and be less dependent on people and possessions.

○ Raphael, the angel of the intellect (Hod), to increase your concentration, improve your memory and be more receptive to new ideas.

○ Uriel, the angel of instinct (Nezah), when you need to get in touch with your sensual nature. Meditating on this aspect can be particularly helpful if you need to resolve guilt issues concerning your sexuality or if you are acutely self-conscious.

○ Michael, the angel of beauty (Tiferet), when you need guidance or comfort or if you find it difficult to empathise with others.

○ Samael, the angel of judgement (Gevurah), when you need to be decisive.

○ Zadkiel, the angel of mercy (Hesed), when you need to practise tolerance, compassion and forgiveness, or if you believe that you are being too self-critical.

○ Zaphkiel, the angel of understanding (Binah), when you are looking for insight into a particular problem.

○ Raziel, the angel of wisdom (Hokhmah), when you seek to understand the significance of a difficult situation.

○ Metatron, the angel of the divine will (Keter), when you seek inspiration and enlightenment.

The four worlds

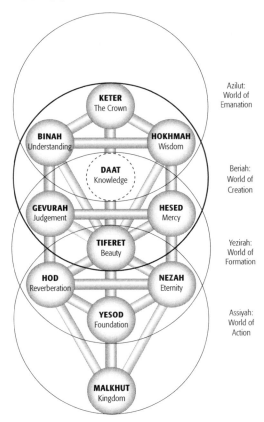

According to Kabbalah, every atom and element in the universe is an expression of the Divine, whose descent into matter is symbolised in a sequence of interpenetrating and interdependent worlds in descending order of manifestation (see the diagram above and on page 120). These are the worlds of Emanation (Azilut: the divine realm of pure consciousness), Creation (Beriah: the realm of spirit presided over by the archangels), Formation (Yezirah: the astral or emotional realm inhabited by the lesser angels) and Action (Assiyah: our physical world). As an embodiment of the Divine we have a spiritual essence, an active intellect, an emotional or astral body and a physical form which enables us to access all four worlds. Practical Kabbalah is concerned with developing a heightened awareness of each of these states and the elements within them so as to sustain a continual sense of the upper worlds whilst cultivating a compassionate detachment from the material world.

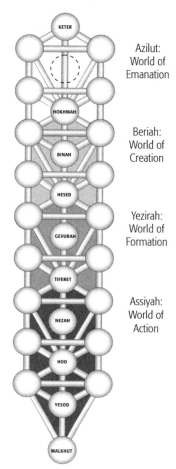

Azilut:
World of
Emanation

Beriah:
World of
Creation

Yezirah:
World of
Formation

Assiyah:
World of
Action

Humans can also be seen as a representation of the four worlds in microcosm.

Exercise: Accessing the angelic realm

To finish our journey through the four worlds we shall close with a traditional Kabbalistic exercise, which will help you to experience the various levels of awareness in order of ascent to the Divine.

Close your eyes and relax by focusing on the rhythm of your breath. Consider your breath as the element of Air and begin by visualising the vital role it plays in the life cycle of the Earth. As you breathe out carbon dioxide, the plants and trees breathe it in and then exude oxygen for you to inhale. Affirm in words of your own choosing that all forms of life on Earth are dependent one upon the other.

Now become conscious of your bones and the skeletal structure which supports the muscles and facilitates movement. Consider your bones as the Earth element in your body.

Then expand your awareness into the natural world and consider the element of Earth in the form of the minerals and nutrients which nurture and nourish the growing plants in the soil: the very same minerals that exist in your bones.

Now become conscious of the blood circulating through your veins to maintain the flow of oxygen to the vital organs. This is the fluid element of your being.

Now expand your awareness into the natural world and consider the third element of Water in the form of the rain, which replenishes the plants and sustains all forms of animal life. See also the world's great oceans teeming with myriad forms of life, from microscopic plankton to the great whales, the leviathans of the seas.

Next, sense the life force generating heat in your skin and consider this the Fire element of your being. Affirm that your body's ability to regulate its own temperature ensures you can cure yourself of the less serious infections by burning up the rogue cells.

Now expand your awareness into the natural world and consider the fourth element of Fire in the form of the nurturing radiance of the Sun, which ensures the continuation of life.

Now consider the mineral component in your body, which maintains the chemical balance and nourishes the muscles and bones.

Then consider the vegetable component, which governs growth and reproduction.

Next, sense the animal principle, which you exhibit as mobility, vitality, instincts, social needs, cunning and curiosity.

Finally, become aware of your unique, human attributes – memory, reflection, aspiration, imagination and your capacity to expand your awareness beyond your physical body to explore the upper worlds.

You are now going to experience that capacity for expanding consciousness into the angelic realms by projecting your awareness beyond your immediate surroundings.

Visualise yourself standing before the entrance to a cavern illuminated from within by the reflected light of countless crystals. Begin your descent a step at a time down a flight of steps carved out of the stone floor of the mountain. Down, down you go, marvelling all the while at the multi-coloured layers of rock and the fossilised remains of billions of creatures preserved from the earliest days of the Earth's existence.

Down, down deeper and deeper to the very core of the Earth where the basic elements of life bubble in a cauldron of molten rock.

Now you notice a gaping wound in the rock to one side from which comes a draught of cool, fresh sea air. You climb through the fissure and find yourself in a vast cathedral-like cavern filled with a lake which spills out into the sea.

You enter the water and are carried by the current into the dark depths of the ocean where an infinite variety of marine life forms dwell far from the light. Rising higher towards the glittering sunlight on the surface you swim in the warmer waters among the shoals of smaller tropical fish, exotic plants and multi-coloured coral.

Breaking the surface, you emerge among the rocks where the crustaceans exist alongside the amphibians in a realm between water and air.

Wading ashore you come to the marshes inhabited by the reptiles and insects in the realm of weather and climate. As you move further inland, drifting like a cloud across the landscape, you survey the valleys, hills and the patchwork of fields coloured by their crops. Here the cattle graze and birds arc across the sky, moving instinctively as one.

Now rise up and see the world as the birds do. See the earth teeming with humanity in all its variations. Take a moment to watch those who express their creativity through art and those skilled with their hands, those who serve others out of compassion and those who seek to advance our understanding of the world around us.

Now ascend through the black silence of space to a point of light which intensifies in brilliance as you approach, until you see that it is not a star at all but a spiral of light. It is a portal into the angelic world, illuminated by innumerable celestial beings. Allow yourself to be drawn through this tunnel of light and, as you do so, experience the sensation of coming home. Beyond is the world of pure spirit where the evolved souls who have broken free of the wheel of life, death and rebirth are to be found.

At the end of the tunnel a figure awaits radiating unconditional love. It is your guardian angel, the all-knowing, compassionate and immortal aspect of your being. You and your guardian angel are now inseparable, two indivisible aspects of the one divine being.

As one you ascend still higher to the realm of the angelic hosts who oversee the cosmic processes. Look about you and observe the hosts of heaven stretching to the far horizon, to the edge of infinity. Now rise again into the world of the archangels who watch over the spiritual progress of humanity.

You are now in the realm of pure consciousness where you can experience the inexpressible beauty and perfection of the angelic realm. Your long journey is at an end. Linger here as long as you wish. Ask for guidance, healing or the clearing of karmic debt. Or simply enjoy the sheer state of bliss which exists at this level of consciousness and be reassured that you are not alone. Know that separation from the source is an illusion.

Bathe in the light and absorb whatever you need at this moment from the eternal light of the Divine. Ask what you will and it will be granted.

The Last Judgement by Gustave Doré

When you are ready, gently descend from the divine dimension, through the tunnel of light into the serenity of space. Pass the planets of our solar system and draw near to the Earth. Descend through the clouds, pass over the oceans and return to the place where you began your journey in spirit. Gradually become aware of your surroundings and the sense of your body in the chair. And when you are ready, open your eyes.

Sit quietly for a few moments assimilating the experience, then stamp your feet to ground yourself.

A Parting Thought

The American writer Sophy Burnham, author of *A Book of Angels,* has recorded a traditional tale which gives an insight into human nature and our relationship with the angels.

She describes how the gods created humankind for their amusement, but first they had to decide where they would hide so that the humans wouldn't find them and spoil the fun. If they hid beneath the waves, some would learn to swim to seek out their creators in the depths. If they hid on the moon they foresaw a time when we would eventually develop rockets in order to seek them out. Nowhere would they be safe so long as man remained insatiably curious about his origins and the nature of the universe.

Finally, the goddess of wisdom came up with the perfect solution. They would hide in the hearts of men, because that is the one place we would never think of looking for them.

May the angels watch over you and your loved ones and draw nearer to us all.

Paul Roland

Recommended Reading

Alma, Daniel, *Ask Your Angels*, Piatkus, 1992
Burnham, Sophy, *A Book of Angels*, Rider, 1992
Goddard, David, *The Sacred Magic of the Angels*, Samuel Weiser, 1996
Halevi, Z'ev ben Shimon, *A Kabbalistic Universe*, Gateway, 1988
Halevi, Z'ev ben Shimon, *The Work of the Kabbalist*, Gateway, 1988
Moolenburgh, Dr H.C., *A Handbook of Angels*, C.W. Daniel, 1988
Moolenburgh, Dr H.C., *Meetings With Angels*, C.W. Daniel, 1992
Ravenwolf, Silver, *Angels Companions in Magick*, Llewellyn, 1997
Rodway, Howard, *Tarot of the Old Path*, AGM, Agmuller, Switzerland, 1990
Roland, Paul, *How To Meditate*, Octopus, 1999
Roland, Paul, *Investigating the Unexplained*, Piatkus, 2000
Roland, Paul, *How Psychic Are You?*, Hamlyn, 2003
Roland, Paul, *Kabbalah – A Piatkus Guide*, Piatkus, 1999
Taylor, Terry Lynn, *Messengers of Light*, HJ Kramer Inc., 1990
White, Ruth, *Working with Guides and Angels*, Piatkus, 1996

Index

126